Advance Praise

"Join Roselee's mesmerizing and relatable journey as she pursues validation in her life-long ambition to be a successful actress —beyond the attention, accolades, and recognition that her artistic life bestowed upon her during a decades-long effort to attain her life's passion. Fueled by the author's relentless drive and fiercely competitive nature, fame eludes this multi-talented artist until she comes to terms with her trajectory as she mourns her mother, raises her beloved son, and reevaluates the true meaning of a successful creative life. *Curtains up on this entertaining, authentic, and riveting memoir. Fasten your seatbelt and take an engaging ride!*"

 —Bara Swain, *award-winning playwright and Creative Consultant, Urban Stages*

"The reminder that an artist just lives to do their best work, just lives for the sake of a creative life regardless of whether it will bring fame brought tears to my eyes. It had so much truth and a profound understanding of the need to fulfill the insane and blessed calling we have. *A beautiful, moving, intelligent, humorous, truthful, and fantastic journey.*"

 —Diane Ciesla, *actress*

"Roselee Blooston tells how she lost her way as an actor and found herself as a writer in this *honest, touching, beautifully written memoir* of her life in the theater."

—*Lucile Lichtblau, nationally-produced playwright*

'A truthful and poignant look at our former selves. *Every artist can relate. Beautifully crafted. Written with skill and emotional intelligence.* This memoir affirms our journey. We, like Blooston, put ourselves courageously to the task. *Almost* is our story."

—*Susan Borofsky, actress, director, and international recording artist*

"*Almost: My Life in the Theater* is a wonderful, beautifully written anatomy of success and failure, how we think about them and how we define ourselves based on them. It is honest, relatable, and very human—whether you aspire to a career in the theater or not—and the anecdotes related are, by turns, sweet and eye-popping. Ms. Blooston namedrops by sharing her brush with fame and the results are hilarious, surprising, and poignant. *A joy to read, who knew a theater memoir could be a page-turner?*"

— *Suzanne Trauth,* author of the novel What Remains of Love, the Dodie O'Dell Mystery Series, award-winning plays, co-author of Sonia Moore and American Acting Training

Almost:
My Life in the Theater

Almost: My Life in the Theater

On ambition, failure, and the drive to create

a memoir

Roselee Blooston

Apprentice House Press
Loyola University Maryland

Copyright © 2022 by Roselee Blooston

All rights reserved. No part of this book may be reproduced or transmitted in any form or by any means, electronic or mechanical, including photocopy, recording, or any information storage and retrieval system, without prior permission from the publisher (except by reviewers who may quote brief passages).

First Edition

Casebound ISBN: 978-1-62720-409-5
Paperback ISBN: 978-1-62720-410-1
Ebook ISBN: 978-1-62720-411-8

Design by Sienna Whalen, Tyler Zorn & Apprentice House Press
Editorial Development by Natalie Misyak
Author photograph taken by Maureen Gates
Cover photograph, the author in *The Trojan Women*,
   American Repertory Theatre of Europe, 1970

Author's Notes:
Some names have been changed.
The word definitions are from Merriam-Webster.com.

"Theater" will sometimes be spelled "theatre," if, for instance, a company or location uses that spelling. I have always preferred the American "er" ending, and so have chosen to use it here, unless such conditions apply.

Published by Apprentice House Press

Loyola University Maryland
4501 N. Charles Street, Baltimore, MD 21210
410.617.5265 • www.ApprenticeHouse.com • info@ApprenticeHouse.com

Also by Roselee Blooston

Dying in Dubai
Trial by Family
The Chocolate Jar and Other Stories

In memory of my mother, Leone Isaacs Blooston,
who believed in the centrality of the arts
&
For Oliver,
whose idea this was

Ever tried. Ever Failed.
No matter. Try again.
Fail again. Fail Better.
— Samuel Beckett

The whole matter…is far simpler than we have made it. It consists of nothing but being able to look straight ahead and see that there could not possibly be any other way.
— Grandfather Tartoni, high-wire artist

Calling

A strong inner impulse toward a particular course for action especially when accompanied by conviction of divine influence

1.

Mother and I sat side by side on the linoleum floor of our Virginia kitchen, with our hands covered in purple and red paint. We were finger-painting. I crouched over the big sheets of glossy white paper in front of us. She sat sidesaddle with her feet tucked under her and slashed the page with a swoop of her hand. I, more tentative, put my two hands on the paper and then "washed" it from top to bottom, creating matching streaks. I don't know how long we went at it, but the memory is indelible. My mother, a bona fide professional artist—she was part of the renowned art movement, the Washington Color School, and her work had been shown at the Corcoran Gallery of Art in Washington, D.C.—and me, a two-year-old with no credentials other than promise, were equals that afternoon, equals in creativity. I remember our joint concentration on filling the page, on making something. Even finger-painting, lowliest of visual art forms, deserved serious consideration. I received the message: all art, whether created on the kitchen floor or in a studio, merited our time and energy. She didn't have to say so. The intention radiated from her to me.

Much later, when I was old enough to understand, Mother explained that she considered the arts—music, writing, dance, visual art, and theater—to be the highest forms of expression and the highest aspirations. Her own gifts as a painter went dormant once she married and had three children—I was the eldest—but she believed fervently in the traditional generational Jewish progression: tradesmen, businessmen, lawyers and doctors, scientists, philosophers, and finally, the pinnacle, artists. She married a lawyer, and saw her children as destined to fulfill the final phase.

That calling—a combination of drive and artistry—was in our DNA. Her mother, my grandmother, had talent too; she sang beautifully. I believed in a non-religious version of "divine influence," *destiny*, and in my artistic inheritance, the direct line between my musical grandmother, my artist mother, and me. Each of us had a calling, a drive to create children, art, and lives.

When, shortly after my first painting experience, I pointed at Captain Kangaroo on television and said, "I want to do *that*," she took me seriously. She understood that I didn't want to be a mustache-sporting gentleman talking to hand puppets. I wanted to live in the make-believe. I wanted to act. Many mothers enrolled their children in dance and art and drama classes to round out their educations, but mine believed in my calling, for its own sake, from the beginning. I started in dance class, curling on the floor in a toddler version of Graham technique. When I was five, Mother noted how well I spoke, and took me to drama class.

I didn't go into the theater to please my mother, but without her validation, I might have hedged my bets and gone straight into teaching. My life in theater would not have been possible without her, and it began on the kitchen floor with a lesson on the value of artistic pursuit for its own sake.

Professional

A person engaged or qualified in a profession; a person competent or skilled in a particular activity—Ex. "she was a real professional on stage"

2.

I made my stage debut in a production of *Around the World in Eighty Days*—my one scene took place in a train going west. Backstage, Mother tied my bonnet and fluffed my long prairie skirt. I knelt on the ground when the train was "attacked." I don't recall any lines, but the vivid life under the lights hooked me in a way watching a television show could not. Time stopped. My intense focus on what I and the rest of the cast were doing, the audience's focus on us, and our shared suspension of disbelief rendered this pretend world more real than reality. An actress I would be.

By age nine, my family had moved to a hilly tree-lined street in Somerset, a quiet neighborhood subsection of Chevy Chase, Maryland, and a close suburb of Washington, D.C., only a mile from the District line. I enrolled in acting classes at the Washington Theater Club, run by a formidable woman in her fifties, Hazel

Wentworth, who happened to live up the street. More than a club, the group housed a professional theater and an acting school but was named to avoid Washington's strict zoning rules. Mrs. Wentworth also directed plays for the Montgomery County Players, a local community theater group. She was about to produce an English drawing room comedy, *Roar Like a Dove* by Lesley Storm, and told my mother that she needed a girl to play Jane, the eldest of six unseen daughters. I auditioned in Mrs. Wentworth's dark, heavily upholstered living room, and got the part.

Rehearsals were at night, sometimes past my bedtime, because everyone in the cast, except me, had day jobs. I of course, had school. My part involved several scenes. I remember the adult actors looming over me, stumbling over their lines, while I knew mine perfectly.

At the dress rehearsal, Mrs. Wentworth told my mother, "Roselee is the only child, and the only professional here." This struck me, though I didn't know what "professional" meant. Now, decades later, I see the statement as the first of many like it that acknowledged my discipline and skill, which overmatched the situation I was in—unpaid, underpaid, and/or amateur.

The opening night went smoothly, until, in a surprise move, Mrs. Wentworth sent me out for my curtain call with five girls in tow, arranged in descending order of height. The audience laughed. My mother fumed. *How dare that woman diminish her daughter's hard-earned moment of reward with a cheap sight gag?* The next performance the children were nowhere to be found, and I got my solo curtain call.

I should say that my mother, fierce in my defense

though she could be, was no stage mom. She was quite shy, didn't drive, and had my brother and sister to take care of, so she couldn't, even if she had wanted to, have become Mama Rose, the toxic, frustrated mama bear from my favorite musical, *Gypsy*. Naming me after my paternal grandmother Rose *and* the notorious stripper Gypsy Rose Lee, whose life story the musical told, comprised the full extent of my mother's foray into stage motherhood.

"Gypsy had a genius IQ," Mother would say, conferring on me a mixed bag of confusion: *be free on stage, brilliant in the classroom, and conforming at home.*

Roar Like a Dove was the first and last community theater production I would act in. From then on, I knew the difference between amateur and professional. Or thought I did. As I said, I kept making the same mistake in different forms, but I understood, even as a child, that professional meant more than money. It meant dedication and competence.

I continued to take classes at the Washington Theater Club, which presented new work and top actors. René Auberjonois performed there, and Roscoe Lee Browne. I loved the classes and was earnest and committed to the plays, but I was also a child, capable of misbehavior. One day before class, another girl and I decided to play hooky, hiding in the ladies' room by standing on top of the toilet seats. The teacher and Mrs. Wentworth called out to us. We didn't answer or giggle. Discipline and control indeed. Mrs. Wentworth called my parents. Then I heard someone say, "We have to call the police." The theater club bordered a dangerous neighborhood. My friend and I came out of the bathroom, heads down, mortified. When my father arrived, he shook, his face ashen. In his low, lightly accented voice—he had immigrated from Poland—he choked out, "Never, ever do that again."

At home, my mother went further, her fear and fury uncontained. "How could you do such a thing? Your father could have had a heart attack. He was so upset." Years later, I realized that any parent would have reacted that way, but my father, who had lost his whole family in the Holocaust, was particularly vulnerable to loss, or even the threat of it. I vowed to become the perfectly behaved child from then on.

My mischief didn't prevent my theater club drama teacher from casting me as the lead in the class play—an original take on *Alice in Wonderland*. I felt the full responsibility of my position. During the entire production, I never left the stage. Again, the bright lights, concentrated space, the laser-like concentration of the audience on everything I did, big or small, and the intoxicating magic of real make-believe cemented my love of acting and of theater. This was my world. This was where I belonged.

Nevertheless, I didn't act again until my senior year in high school. My parents were alarmed by my misery in the local public high school in Bethesda, Maryland. I had been shut out of the extremely cliquey drama program, and rather than fight to break through, I retreated into myself—writing bad poetry, painting, and daydreaming about the stage.

I spent the summer between my junior and senior years in Interlochen, Michigan at its famed National

Music Camp, where I majored in art and minored in drama; it should have been the other way around, but my confidence was shaken by my high school experience. The camp's Oral Interpretation teacher wrote me a recommendation for the Interlochen Arts Academy, a new boarding school for young artists, and at the end of the summer, knowing I was about to embark on a full year there, gave me a book of poetry with the inscription: *to Roselee, who will always do more than expected.*

My Academy drama instructor told me that I was "too intelligent" to be an actress and suggested directing as an alternative. I wouldn't hear of it. But I was acutely aware of who the class stars were—not me—and remained utterly intimidated by them throughout my time there. Alma, a statuesque blond with a sultry voice beyond her years, was considered the strongest actress and a sure bet to "make it." She exuded so much charisma that she had a groupie, a sophomore who followed her around like a puppy. No one thought much of this short, odd-looking boy, who became, fifteen years later, an Oscar-nominated actor for the title role in *Amadeus*. The boy's name: Tom Hulce.

Tom's ascendancy from nerdy undeveloped teenager to world-wide recognition taught me my first lesson in the unpredictability of fame. No one at Interlochen in 1970 would have bet on him. Everyone had their money on Alma and a couple of other bright lights headed for Juilliard. Not one of them was heard from again. One became a nurse, one a pilot, and Alma…*who knows?* I wish her well, and hope that she has made peace with her version of *almost*.

3.

The summer between my graduation from Interlochen and my first year in college, I joined the American Repertory Theater in Europe, affiliated with the American School in Switzerland, to tour two classical plays to outdoor venues including ancient amphitheaters in Italy and Greece. It was an exhilarating, heady experience for a seventeen-year-old only a month out of high school. The other members of the company were all older—college students and West Coast grad students—far more worldly than I.

For ten weeks, my only means of communication with my family in the States was by letter.

July 3, 1970

Dear Mommy and Daddy,

Well, I told you I was out for blood, and I got it! A lead in Lysistrata—Myrrhine, the part I wanted. I have the key scene in the play! In The Trojan Women I have the solo part in the chorus. All of my talents seem to have fallen into place here. My comic sense got me the part in Lysistrata. The directors said that my 'beautifully strong voice' and my emotional concentration cinched the part in The Trojan Women. I sound conceited, don't I? It's really just the shock of being sure again of my calling.

That cockiness masked tremendous fear. I didn't want my parents to worry, so I told them only what I thought they would want to hear. Under my bravura, I was shaky. At first, this recognition and responsibility—they thought I was talented enough to handle two leads—played into my grandiose self-image as a precocious-mature-beyond-her-years actress-student-young woman. Then came the crash.

July 15, 1970

These past 2 weeks have really been something and yesterday was quite a climax. We had run-throughs of both plays, one right after another. Everyone has been getting colds, coughs, and general nervous fatigue. I, for one, had seen enough and decided to speak up. The directors were impressed that I was honest enough to tell them what was happening. During our conversation, they said something that really floored me: whether I knew it or not, I am ready for this experience, that to most of the students it will mean little or nothing, but to me it will be invaluable. I am made for what I am doing.

Translation: afraid that I would fail, I cried to the directors that I couldn't play both parts, the pressure was too much. They listened and calmed me down, told me how well I was doing and that they knew I'd be fine. These two men understood that I was homesick and freaked out by the older, more socially sophisticated group. That very morning, a rehearsal kiss from my *Lysistrata* husband became my first kiss ever, a sloppy one, in front of a cast of strangers—not how I'd envisioned this romantic milestone. The play was about women going on a sex strike to stop their men from going to war, but I was the proverbial babe in the woods. I may have been ready for the work, but I wasn't ready for the life.

And then there was the seduction scene in *Lysistrata*. To appease Italy's Catholic sensibilities, my costume for the strip tease was a nun's idea of a bikini: white granny panties covering my navel and a surgical bra. Unflattering to say the least. It would have made Gypsy Rose Lee gag. *How would I live up to my infamous namesake as my mother expected, and still retain my virginity, also expected?* I resolved to be bold on stage and reserved off.

I descended stone stairs flooded with light in Fiesole's amphitheater outside Florence—remove belt, pause, smile, pause, flirt with my hubby, begging on his knees, pause, remove top of shift, pause, reveal bra, pause, drop dress, pause, reveal bottoms. In rehearsal I had been keenly self-conscious about my ample thighs but brazened through the routine like the trouper I considered myself to be. The non-English speaking audience roared. *Were they laughing at me or with me?* Probably both. In contrast, for the Euripides, I wore black, unrevealing robes, while I ripped my vocal cords by shouting over the whipping winds in Les Baux de Provence, with its ruins as back drop, bloodying my knees on the dirt and rocks. Out-of-body experiences and a theatrical coming of age.

Afterwards, I felt ready for anything and certainly for college. Fiercely competitive, I knew that this experience would put me ahead of the pack.

4.

In the fall of 1970, I tried out for my first play at Vassar College, where I was an entering freshman who had been awarded sophomore standing, due to the Advanced Placement credits that I had amassed during my year at the Interlochen Arts Academy. Along with the actual credits, that year gave me, unlike most freshman, substantial acting training.

When I found out that Vassar's first show would be *Lysistrata*, I thought, *piece of cake*. Of course, I tried out for Myrrhine, and made it clear that I knew the part inside out. The director, Clint Atkinson, was impressed, though I didn't get the role. Instead, he cast me as leader of the women's chorus, not knowing that I had experience in that vein as well. He put the choruses in old age masks and dressed the women in bikinis—real ones this time. Talk about déjà vu! I wore my green paisley two-piece threaded with silver, which sparkled in the stage lighting, and once again, tried to forget about my thighs. I had to make out on stage with the leader of the men's chorus; blinded by lust, I promptly developed a wild crush on him, which went nowhere.

While at Vassar, I became thoroughly entrenched in the world of drama majors. Drama departments are hierarchical places, especially ones as small as this. As soon as I won a major role, word got around that an uppity freshman had taken what should have gone to an upperclassman. After meeting the rest of the *Lysistrata* cast, I heard mention that everyone had thought the title role would go to a senior with the unusual name, Meryl Streep. Clint—we didn't call him "professor," just "Clint"—had discovered Meryl, and cast her a couple of years earlier in a now legendary production of Strindberg's *Miss Julie*. Everyone who saw her performance asked, *who was this incandescent presence gracing the Vassar stage?*

Clint, a professional New York director, and a big bear of a man with twinkling eyes and a sharp wit, held a central role in the lives of all of us who aspired to a career in the theater. Clint had other plans for Meryl than tackling Aristophanes. Later that year, she played the lead in *The London Merchant*, a forgettable play with an unforgettable leading lady. *The Poughkeepsie Journal* raved, "Her voice is exquisite, her face expressive and her theatrics superb." Since I wasn't in her show, or on one of the backstage crews that fall and winter, I only saw glimpses of magical Meryl. She seemed to be merely an unusually mature-looking student—blond, pale, with a patrician nose and long neck, elegant more than pretty, a woman, while we were merely girls. Then I saw her act. Instantly, I understood. She was undeniably magnetic, completely free on stage, while at the same time in total control: a true leading lady. Even then, a star.

The final production of my first year in college was Tennessee Williams' *Camino Real*, The play had a huge cast—a plus for college directors trying to satisfy a lot of eager and frustrated acting students—and served as Meryl's senior project. She would design all the costumes. Not only was she a fine actress, but she was also a gifted designer. I played a stuffy English woman, yet another old lady character part, already my niche. Meryl dressed me in a pastel suit and a large, feathered hat. Still, I had no contact with her until the first dress rehearsal. I sat downstage left at a café table, as Meryl approached me from below—the proscenium stage was at least a couple feet above her. She wanted me to tilt my hat to make my face fully visible. Meryl moment number one.

In the fall of my second year at Vassar, Clint cast me in the title role of *Lady Precious Stream*, a reworked Chinese fairy tale about a long-suffering wife whose husband left her for decades, an Asian Penelope and Odysseus. Its set and costumes were the most memorable thing about the production. Our tie-dyed robes and pajama pants swirled with soft colors. The backdrop consisted of a curtain of woven plastic, fashioned entirely out of six-pack holders—material easily procured on a college campus years before recycling became a requirement. The crew joked that they were drinking for their art. The headdresses too, were woven out of the same and placed over papier-mâché bases. The whole effect could have gone very wrong. Without theatrical lighting the curtain and headdresses looked absurd, like a stoner's arts and crafts project, but once lit, they glistened, creating a delicate fantasy world perfect for the sentimental tale.

Lady Precious Stream marked my first lead role at college, and like the coup of landing a major supporting role as a freshman, this was also a big vote of confidence from Clint, who directed both. He told me that he had picked the show for me.

Much later, as a long-married woman whose husband traveled a great deal, I realized that Clint had seen something elemental in my nature, an innocence, and a traditional steadfastness, quite out of sync with the free-love environment in which I came of age. I was raised by strict old-fashioned parents who told me in no uncertain terms that I had to remain "intact," or they would refuse to fund my education. *How would they have known?* Only if I told them. But I was so cowed, that I believed them.

Virginity aside, I was entirely convincing as a married woman who would wait faithfully *for years*—without word or sign from her husband—for him to return. Ugh. My real-life version of the patient spouse, keeping the home fires burning, would be a much greater torment than the dramatic fiction, so much so that I wrote a memoir about it.

Because I was required to take Intro to Acting, I

never had the dubious pleasure of taking class from the great film star and Oscar nominee, Jean Arthur. I say "dubious," because, as my friends told me, she didn't so much teach as demonstrate. When a scene went awry, she got on stage and proceeded to *play* the part all the way through. By that time, she was in her late sixties and the scenes, obviously, centered around young characters. My classmates considered her course torture.

Ms. Arthur was also a recluse. She didn't go to faculty meetings or hold office hours. She taught her classes and retreated to her off-campus home. Nor did she direct productions or come to public performances. She did, however, attend the dress rehearsal of *Lady Precious Stream*. I remember a lone, small—she was five feet tall, about my height—pixyish figure with short white hair, standing in the back corner of the empty auditorium throughout the full-length show, as if she would bolt at any moment. As soon as the rehearsal ended and we gathered on the edge of the stage for notes, she disappeared. Later, Clint told me that Ms. Arthur, who almost never commented on department productions, had said, "that girl knows what she is doing." I took it as high praise and stored it away.

But it was Meryl moment number two—during my own senior year, with Meryl long gone—that stayed with me, guided me, changed me, and later tormented me. That moment came just before graduation, as the gang and I sat in the theater auditorium watching a tech rehearsal for *Dames at Sea*, a fellow classmate's senior project.

I had already completed my own very ambitious project, a full production of Samuel Beckett's *Happy

Days, in which I played Winnie, who spent the entire first act buried up to her waist in sand, and the second, buried up to her neck." Diane Wiest, who played the role in 2016, called it "Hamlet for actresses." I had a lot of nerve, that was for sure.

I didn't know it then, but that marathon monologue set me on my solo performance path. I learned then that I could hold the stage by myself, and I loved it—the concentrated energy, power, and control—and the secure freedom of losing myself within the limits of the script. I experienced all of this in ensemble productions too, but the risk of standing—or in this case, sitting—alone in front of an audience, knowing what would happen, yet not knowing entirely, because each performance was unique, fueled me most. I felt most fully alive on stage; I lived for the next "curtain up."

That day, before the *Dames* rehearsal, Clint came over—he was the musical's advisor—and we began grilling him about our collective prospects. After all, he was our link to the professional theater world and all of us were anxious about the future. Clint was a sharp, funny, no-nonsense director. We worshipped him. We would miss him. Now we wanted him to tell us the truth.

Someone—I don't remember who—asked, "Who among us do you think could have a *real* acting career? Tell us, we can take it."

Clint sat on the aisle, perched on top of one of the seats. He shook his head. "You really want to know?" he said. We nodded. "Meryl," he said without hesitation. It was a given that she was destined for greatness.

"Of course, course. Besides Meryl," we chimed.

Then he looked me in the eye. "And Roselee. Meryl and Roselee."

I blushed.

Everyone was silent. The tech resumed. No one ever discussed it. At that point we didn't really know what it meant.

I was stunned. This was big.

Over the following years, as Meryl's career skyrocketed, and mine stalled, I thought, *but Clint said...* and I kept going. For decades, watching her amass Oscar after Oscar, I believed that my version of success as an actor was just around the corner. *Clint said.*

I want to note here that many others in the class of '73 had careers on Broadway, in film, television, commercials, and voice-overs—much, much bigger and more successful careers than mine. They became working professional actors, despite not having been anointed that day by our teacher.

Whenever a new Meryl movie came out, two of my Vassar classmates and I would meet to see it. We gazed in awe as she dominated in *Doubt,* and laughed uproariously when she pranced and sang in *Mamma Mia!* We still gossiped about her. She was part of our early bond. She connected us. Always, in my mind, behind each of these encounters with the by then world-class myth of Meryl were Clint's words: a compliment, a vote of confidence from a respected theater teacher and director, and gradually over time, a taunt: *What's wrong with you? You had it, and you failed.*

I've never told this story publicly before. Only my husband and my closest friends and family ever heard me talk about my failure to live up to the "Meryl and me" prediction. *And my therapist.* Thirty-three years later, ten years after I had left acting for good, I sat in therapy and talked about my tremendous potential and my disappointing trajectory. By then, I had accepted that I wouldn't fulfill Clint's prophesy, though I still hadn't accepted that I could or should redefine my actual accomplishments as well-earned and even desirable. Instead, I'd been haunted by those fateful words of encouragement.

I came to realize that I was not only a very talented girl, but also one with a passion to express her deepest self, a drive that couldn't mesh with the business of theater. Whenever I had a choice about where to put my energies, I chose art and personal meaning over a more strategic move. Eventually I understood that I was stuck in a tape that was no longer useful or healthy. I needed to accept reality: Meryl was an international star, the greatest actress of our generation, and I was not. *Not even close.*

Jean Arthur had not only commented on my abilities, but also on Meryl's. "It was like watching a movie star," said the actress who was one.

5.

For two summers, during college and immediately after graduation, I had the old-fashioned pleasure of doing summer stock at the Monomoy Theater in Chatham, Massachusetts on Cape Cod—old-fashioned, because today there are fewer and fewer viable summer theaters where young actors can learn their craft in front of live, paying audiences, let alone perform in eight plays in as many weeks—most of them classics, from Shakespeare to Neil Simon, with one big musical to round out the season.

Like my opportunities at Vassar, this one came from Clint. When he wasn't in Poughkeepsie teaching, he directed in New York City at the Equity Library Theater, where he met the daughter of Christopher Lane, the Monomoy's artistic director. The theater's company, the Ohio University Players, came almost exclusively from Ohio University's B.F.A. theater program, but every year had one or two slots for outsiders. The standards were high. A Bachelor of Fine Arts is a professional degree meant to prepare the student for a life in the theater. Vassar, like all liberal arts colleges, offered a Bachelor of Arts with broader requirements, but Clint recommended me, so any doubts that I might not be up to the company's level, vanished. He told me that Monomoy was just what I needed to develop my range.

Next thing I knew, I was introducing myself to the company with a series of auditions—cold readings from the summer's shows—in the living room of the house where we all lived together, adjacent to the theater. The cozy atmosphere and the competitive but supportive directors and actors felt like home. Any intimidation evaporated with my first audition. One of the actors approached me after that first reading and said, "You are excellent."

The smell of sea air and the quaint Cape villages lent a charmed quality to my Monomoy summers. Although the work didn't pay, it didn't cost us anything either. We got room, board, and invaluable pre-professional experience. Unlike the European tour, I fit right in and was ready for the challenge. The schedule exhausted and exhilarated me by turns. We rehearsed one play during the day and performed another play at night.

I was cast as Lucetta in Shakespeare's *Two Gentleman of Verona*, Esther in Arthur Miller's *The Price*, and Jane in Alan Ayckbourn's *Absurd Person Singular*. A pattern emerged: I played character roles, by definition, supporting, i.e., the trusted servant or the middle-aged wife, with the exception of Peggy Evans in Neil Simon's *Come*

Blow Your Horn, in which I had the pleasure of wearing a midriff blouse, tight skirt, and a long ponytail. I spent most of my time on stage chased around the set by Alan Rust, who was playing a womanizer also named Alan.

Alan R. would later become the artistic director of the Monomoy, and in a reunion decades later in the theater's offices, he would point to the ceiling papered with actor headshots from season's past, home in on the girl with the bushy hair and wide eyes, and say, "There you still are!"

Then, however, I focused mostly on trying to appear cool during my second stage kiss, another sloppy one.

My biggest role, Dorine in Moliere's *Tartuffe*, fell into the servant category, with a difference. Dorine was the central foil to the title role, smart enough to see through him and to call his bluff. The play, translated by Richard Wilbur, was written entirely in rhymed couplets, which were much harder to memorize than Shakespeare's iambic pentameter, whose rhythms more closely resembled ordinary speech. On opening night, two cast members—veteran actors, not students—began their scene, and a few lines in, skipped to the end, leaving out crucial information. They panicked. Realizing that there was no way back, without explanation, they exited. I rushed on stage to move the play forward and found myself in scene after scene covering for the holes in my scene partners' memories. Somehow, we made it to the curtain call.

Non-actors tend to think of acting as mostly memorization, and often ask, *how did you learn all those lines?* After my solo stint in *Happy Days*, even fellow student actors, who knew better, asked. I bristled at the suggestion that this was the biggest challenge; it was the job, the most basic requirement. Noel Coward advised actors to "Just say the lines and don't bump into the furniture." But in a play like *Tartuffe* memorization turned into a virtuosic test. I passed. Not only did I find it easy to learn the material, but I loved playing someone as funny, sassy, and strong as Dorine. The reviews were great. This time, unlike the European ones, I could read them.

My parents and sister came to see the show. I was happy to display my prowess in this talented company. I posed for photos next to the billboard outside the theater with "Tartuffe" in ornate lettering. I claimed ownership. This was *my* show.

There were a lot of firsts that summer: I sang my first solo as Frankie of "Frankie and Johnny" in *Of Thee I Sing*. I rehearsed the song non-stop, whenever I was alone, primarily in the shower. I remember the shock of the chesty voice, so unlike my speaking voice, booming out of me—dry and clothed this time—and the faces of the audience. At least I stayed on key. No one got up to leave. And I danced my way through *A Funny Thing Happened on the Way to the Forum*.

I also taught my first class. Kathleen Stafford from the Bristol Old Vic Theater School in England taught a voice class. She came to Chatham every summer and directed the annual Shakespeare productions. A small, wizened woman in her seventies, Ms. Stafford wielded tremendous authority. When she asked me to lead the group's movement warm-ups before her class, I wondered, *why me?* I wasn't one of the BFA actors. I was flattered and a bit daunted. I took what I had learned at Interlochen, Vassar, and on the European tour, and filled my "class" with sun salutations, stretches, dance, and mime. Then Ms. Stafford took over. We were quite a pair: she, an ancient legendary theater teacher and me, a green novice. She saw something in me—future potential, or lack thereof. I would go on to make a living teaching the full range of skills actors needed: scene study, speech, movement, and later playwriting. The saying, *those who can't do, teach,* I would amend to *those who can't make money doing, teach.*

There was fun, too. The first summer, I had a crush on one of the designers, a burly guy with dark curly hair whose girlfriend in the company played the most sophisticated parts. My parents saw the potential and invited him to lunch. Awkward doesn't begin to describe that sit-down.

On the way back to the theater he held my hand. "Be careful," he said. "There are a lot of predatory men in the theater." It was obvious that he didn't think of me as anything but a kid sister.

He also warned me away from the lighting and tech guy I was hanging out with. That attraction—unlike the cerebral one to the designer—was carnal, and apparent to everyone around us. After a show we would sneak off to the beach to make out. When things got too hot, I'd shut it down. Tech had red hair, freckles, and green, dangerous eyes. He smoked, was in his late twenties, and called me "Vassar." A total turn-on. Midway through the summer, his longtime, and I'm afraid, long-suffering, girlfriend showed up. She knew something was going on. I felt guilty, but we hadn't slept together, so I told myself I hadn't done anything wrong. The whole company expected the triangle to blow up in our faces. It didn't. She wanted Tech to marry her. He wanted to play around. With me.

When the season ended, he wrote me letters. "I can't get you out of my mind." I wrote back, telling him to choose her or me. He couldn't and didn't.

The next summer we all came back: me, the designer, and Tech. This time, no action, except on stage.

6.

My summers on the Cape were full of play, on stage and off, but the atmosphere back on campus was tense. Vassar had just gone coed, and the ratio of women to men was about ten to one. I had entered with the first officially coed class, 1974. Due to my accelerated status, I graduated in 1973, with the last *non*-coed class. My undergraduate years bookended the sea change at the college, and, at least socially, were defined by it. Given the dearth of males, my interactions with the opposite sex confined themselves to the stage, rendering them both safe and unreal. In any case, I couldn't deny the physicality, the sensuality of my chosen art form, though for a long time, I had little or no experience outside my craft.

But there was one collegiate incident which haunted me for years, and which only lately, have I understood as formative.

"I'm going to kill you." Tom stood stoned, in the middle of a room full of drama majors, all equally wasted at the cast party for the department's production of *The House of Bernarda Alba*, a depressing ponderous affair.

We were happy the show was over. The all-female cast didn't make for a great party. The few guys who came ran crew—sound, lights, or set. Tom was the stage manager. The men of the class of '74 were an unconventional bunch—mostly sons of alums, gay men, and Vietnam veterans. Almost all of them were spoiled, unavailable, and/or fried. Tom checked the first category and acted like the third. He stared down at me, dead-eyed, his shoulder-length brown hair flopping forward, concealing his long neck. Tom was tall, thin, almost spectral, and possessed an inwardness at odds with the sudden aggression. He was a boy I wouldn't have paid any attention to.

I did a double take. "What did you say?"

The room stank with smoke and reverberated with loud laughter. Tom hadn't taken his eyes off me since I walked in, at least twenty minutes earlier. I sipped my tequila sunrise and asked him again. He said nothing and stepped closer, almost tripping over a freshman who'd played Bernarda's sexy youngest daughter. She sprawled on the floor, still in character, next to the lighting designer, a twenty-eight-year-old—an ancient, as far as we were concerned, burn-out case, who neither shaved his stubble nor grew a beard.

"I'm going to kill you." Tom's unblinking eyes shone like hard, bright marbles. No one else seemed to hear him but me, or if they did, they were too far gone to react. "You should be dead," he said. His body didn't twitch; it was too still. His arms hung from his shoulders like empty sleeves on a hanger.

The haze in the room thickened. The smell of weed made me nauseous. *Or was it the threat?* Bernarda, tall and dour, and her maid, a jolly English girl, who didn't know how not to smile, waved me over to the corner where they were giggling and passing a joint. I didn't move.

Tom grinned. He knew he was getting to me. "Just kidding," he hissed.

My eyes watered from the smoke. Tom had never talked to me before, not through the month of rehearsals, or the week of performances. *Why now? Why this?* I couldn't decide whether to stay or go, join my castmates, pretend nothing was happening, or run back to the dorm and call my father.

I looked at Tom again. We seemed to be stuck in our own separate tunnel. He pointed his finger at me and cocked an invisible trigger.

I don't remember leaving the party, or how I got back to my room. The next thing I recall was a man's voice outside my window, shouting my name. "Roselee!" It was 2 or 3 o'clock in the morning. I inched next to the window, afraid to peek, and pulled back the shade. I'd often imagined my own version of the balcony scene—a suitor singing corny love songs from below. But not this. Not Tom.

"You're dead, Blooston," he called.

I pulled away from the window. I didn't have a

telephone in my room, let alone a cellphone—it was 1972, no one did—and I didn't dare go down to the lobby to the pay phone in case he was waiting for me. I don't know how long Tom stood beneath my window, but I stayed awake, rigid in my bed, until the sun came up.

My father drove from our home in Maryland to campus the next day. He met with the college president and Poughkeepsie's Chief of Police, who promised that his men would go to Tom's apartment and scare the hell out of him. They must have done just that, because Tom never spoke to me or looked at me again.

At the department meeting the following week, all eyes swept back and forth like windshield wipers between Tom and me. Afterwards Clint took me aside. "What happened with Tom?"

I hesitated. I couldn't say "kill" or "dead." Instead, I said, "He threatened me."

"Really?" Clint's reaction wasn't what I needed. I got the feeling that he didn't believe me, that no one did, that they thought poor, innocent, sheltered Roselee was exaggerating, making things up.

The following fall, the Poughkeepsie Police Chief came to see me perform. Afterwards, he asked me out for a drink. Before I got in his car, Clint peered through the window, forehead furrowed. "Are you okay?" I thought, *Sure. I'm with the Chief of Police.* I nodded and we sped away.

He took me to a bar miles from campus and I got

drunk on whiskey and rye, drunker than I'd ever been. A couple hours later, he drove me back to my dorm. Before I could get out of the car, he made a pass at me. More than a pass. He lunged for me over and over. I had to jam the heels of both hands into his chest, push away his stubbly jaw. I held my breath while he exhaled, "Come on honey," in stale wafts of gin and cigarettes. I don't know how I managed to extricate myself from his groping reach except that he was as smashed as I was. I scrambled out of the car. The ground lurched under me, and I zigzagged my way back to my room, holding onto the stair railing with both hands as I climbed to the dorm's second floor.

The Chief called me a few days later, clearly wanting to pick up where we had left off. I didn't answer his suggestion that we go out again but thanked him politely for all he had done. Well, *not all*. The professional part. The entire incident left me, if not physically harmed, then psychologically shaken. *Was this what it meant to be a woman in the world? Was I merely prey of one sort or another?*

Tom's threat and the Chief's inappropriate passes seem quaint in comparison to what can happen on today's college campuses. Menacing words. Drunken groping. Nothing further. But I can still see the scars on the Chief's leathery cheeks and smell his tobacco breath. He scared me way more than Tom had. *How stupid was I to get in that car? How naïve?* It took me a long time to dare to be alone with a man again. I had to relearn how to trust my own instincts.

I didn't tell my parents what had happened until many years after graduation. They needed to believe that I was safe in my prestigious Seven Sisters College with my new private phone, deadbolt, door chain, and under the protection of the town's Chief of Police. I wasn't about to burst their bubble.

Did this encounter contribute to my going solo years later? Maybe. *Did it help set in motion a need to be safe, even if that desire was a subconscious one?* Possibly. I do know that I wanted my voice to be heard, my body to be seen, and my mind and heart to be appreciated as worthy of attention for their intrinsic value, not as subordinate. If there was a way, I was going to eliminate any threat to my prowess. I wanted recognition, beyond my femaleness, for my abilities first, my womanhood second, or not at all. *Impossible?* I could end up isolated, marginalized. Perhaps. But I went for it regardless.

7.

The Dallas Theater Center wasn't my first choice for graduate school after Vassar. Like many aspiring actresses—in the '70s we still called ourselves actresses, though a decade later, "actor" took hold—I wanted to attend Julliard or follow Meryl to the Yale School of Drama. I auditioned for both.

I did an excerpt from *Happy Days*. I figured this tour de force monologue would wow the admissions committees the way it had the Vassar crowd. For my second piece, I chose Imogen from Shakespeare's "Cymbeline." With one summer at the Central School of Speech and Drama in London and two of classical summer stock on Cape Cod behind me, I felt especially able to handle the demands of verse.

I remember Julliard's semi-darkened stage, a deep well surrounded by tiers of seats above. I saw the great Marian Seldes on the left. Her Tony-winning performance in Edward Albee's *A Delicate Balance* had stunned me. John Houseman, the formidable director-producer, long-time collaborator with Orson Wells, and founder of Juilliard's drama division, loomed third-row center. Who can forget Houseman's Oscar-winning turn as the intimidating Professor Kingsfield in the film *The Paper Chase*? That film came out in the fall of '73, months after Juilliard rejected me. I watched the movie, nodding my head. The imposing Kingsfield on screen matched the Houseman I had met.

At Yale the moment I entered the audition room, I knew I was doomed. The intimate space shut me down. I could both disappear and reveal on a stage. In that claustrophobic room, I couldn't. After years of teaching in college and conservatory programs, I realize that both schools probably wanted young actors who weren't hiding behind characters too old and too far from their experience, moldable beings, who also had a spark of originality. I had the latter but wasn't particularly moldable. And then there was the undeniable fact that these top programs were wildly competitive, auditioning hundreds for a few coveted places. Just like the profession itself, landing a spot was a crapshoot.

Clint wrote my recommendations for Julliard and Yale but suggested that I apply to the Dallas Theater Center; he probably understood that disappointment was in the offing. The Texas school was affiliated with Trinity University of San Antonio, and granted an MFA in Drama, a terminal degree equal in the performing arts to a PhD. Clint was right. I applied and was quickly accepted, with a package that included a full fellowship, and jobs teaching children's theater and in the season ticket office—merit money, which amounted to a free ride, unheard of for most theater schools, certainly today. My parents sighed with relief, since my brother was in college and my sister would follow soon. I could pay my own way.

The Dallas Theater Center took a unique approach to actor training; it based its company-led classes on Paul Baker's unique philosophy of creativity. Baker founded and directed the theater and was a genuine maverick in Texas educational and artistic circles. I read his book, *Integration of Abilities: Exercises for Creative Growth*, before applying. Baker embraced all the arts. That resonated, raised as I was by a mother who had done the same. And unlike other Equity regional companies, this group of theater professionals made a living by wearing many hats. It was not unusual to find the lead in the previous evening's main stage play repairing costumes the next day in the basement shop. The entire scenario intrigued me.

Landing in Dallas was like landing in another country. *Where was I?* Texas was and still is a land apart, though depression hung in the city's air. I had arrived exactly ten years after President Kennedy's assassination, and collective guilt covered Dallas like a shroud. I took a taxi from the airport directly to the theater. The landscape looked gray, flat, and at the same time, too bright for my East Coast eyes.

The Theater Center stood out. Designed by Frank

Lloyd Wright in 1959—the only theater among his buildings—it sat tucked away on Turtle Creek Boulevard, a round structure reminiscent of the Guggenheim in New York, like a white womb. I lugged my suitcases into the lobby, exhaled. *Now what?* I had arrived, with no idea where I was going to live.

Another new student and I bonded at the bulletin board, while desperately perusing the listings for apartments. We decided then and there to room together, and quickly found a cheap two-bedroom within walking distance of the theater, a necessity since I didn't have a car.

That roommate, a wealthy Texas girl—the daughter of an oil magnate—took issue with the fact that I wasn't into partying and wasn't interested in the short boys who were attracted to me. She needed a posse, and I wouldn't join.

On Thanksgiving she threw a dinner for those of us who couldn't go home. We waited hours for her father's private plane to land with the turkey. By the time he showed up, we had eaten all the sides and desserts, too full for another bite. In January I moved to an apartment of my own in the same complex.

Roommate troubles aside, I loved the classes and productions. In Mr. Baker's Theatre Philosophy class, based on his book, he used me as an example of creative processes: "This young lady, for instance, looks at a problem, immediately gives it a form, puts a box around it, shakes it for a while and solves it." I felt seen.

The first year I won the coveted role of Mary Warren in *The Crucible*, beating out several actresses who had been at the DTC longer. It would be a main stage show for the Center's subscription audience. This part, in a respected regional theater production, marked my first professional role.

My entrance, along with the other girls in the cast, was from above the stage, swinging down on heavy ropes and landing "in the woods" to dance. I found the action surprisingly bracing; my usual fear of heights disappeared. I loved the wildness and freedom of those few seconds in the air and the power of all eyes on me, a high, both literal and figurative.

As in college, where I packed four years into three, I rushed to finish the three-year MFA program in two, for no other reason than that I could. Along with my friend Celeste, I won DTC's highest student honor: the Greer Garson Theater Arts Award. The then seventy-year-old Miss Garson lived in Dallas. She would present the award certificate and a small honorarium to us in person. My parents were over the moon. They had admired her in *Mrs. Miniver*, her Oscar winning performance. To them, the award meant that I, too, was destined to become a star. And what they believed, I believed. She and I also shared a birthdate, September 29th—another sign cementing our kinship.

The day of the presentation I waited nervously in the auditorium to greet the great lady. She did not disappoint. When Greer Garson entered, accompanied by Mr. Baker, she exuded old school Hollywood glamour. Though it rarely dropped below 60 degrees in Dallas, she wore a white wool coat with a giant fur collar, which she did not remove. Her perfectly coiffed signature flame red hair blazed. Her hands were adorned with chunky jeweled rings, and she had tied a turquoise scarf loosely around her white turtleneck. Even with all that carefully chosen attire, it was her eyes, not the lashes or make-up or clothing, but her huge green eyes that struck me, with their extraordinary depth and magnetism.

I heard my name, stood up, stepped onto the stage, received the award, and shook Miss Garson's hand. Later, Celeste and I flanked her on either side in the theater lobby, posing for a photograph. The movie star didn't speak to us, either on stage or off. She knew the focus was on her and didn't expend energy on anything but her own radiant composure. My mother had the award and the picture framed in gold gilt. It still hangs in my study.

I was an excellent student—dedicated, and serious. My second year acting teachers commenting on my Mary Tyrone from *Long Day's Journey into Night*—yet another old lady role—called it "brilliant," thanked me for the experience, said that I made them feel "inadequate," and that I should play the part one day, age be damned. I thought, *something to look forward to*. But the world of school, even in this hands-on regional-theater-cum-grad-school, wasn't the real world. In the real world, being a great student wouldn't be enough.

A few months after the award, I, along with the other Theater Center graduates, performed practice auditions for a company member who ran a non-Equity bus and truck touring company. He offered me a job—the only offer he made. Unfortunately, it didn't include a living wage. The contract required me to pay for my own transportation to and from the rehearsal site in Texas and to sew all the company costumes. Alas, I wasn't much of a seamstress. I turned it down, sure that there would be many more and better jobs, and that this was yet another sign I could work in the industry.

Today, I look at the framed photograph on my study wall, at the chubby cheeked twenty-two-year-old, standing next to a film legend, and think, *this was one of the highlights of my life*. I didn't know then that an auspicious beginning is no guarantee of success.

I did a lot of growing up in grad school, but continued to guard my virginity, even though my parents could no longer hold tuition over my head. I had some heavy flirtations with company members and students, but my big Dallas romance was with a beautiful man, Ray, who looked like a cross between Clark Gable and Omar Sharif. He sported a mustache, always behaved as a gentleman—my mother labeled his manners "too perfect"—and was as sensitive a friend as a girl could want. He took me to the doctor when I wrenched my back during a rehearsal, drove me to San Antonio for my MFA orals, and listened for hours to my worries about the future. The only trouble: he was gay. We both knew that our attraction was real—hours of making out proved as much—and that it couldn't go anywhere. Nevertheless, we stuck together, giving each other comfort and an accepting ear. From time to time, I cooked for him. One night over dinner, he put down his fork, looked up at me, and said, "You will make someone a good wife someday."

I sigh thinking of the small irony that it would be my husband Jerry who did the best cooking in our home.

After I left Dallas to go home to Maryland, Ray and I wrote each other letters. Until my parents put a stop to it. They couldn't understand a love that didn't fit their preconceptions—especially my father, who couldn't make the connection between the value he and my mother had placed on my virtue and my ingenious solution: the love of a gay man. When I confronted Daddy, he said, "What's wrong with you? Why haven't you had sex yet?" completely disavowing his part in the virgin-whore dichotomy he'd long promoted. At this point my mother backed off, but the damage was done. When I did what I was told to do by the people in whose house I now resided, and wrote to Ray not to contact me again, I hurt my friend. Badly.

A year later, I returned to Texas for my first teaching job at the University of Texas in Austin. Ray visited me. We walked the sprawling campus, talked about our goals—like old times. I apologized. He said he understood. I'm sure he did. He had faced more rejection in his life than I could have ever imagined.

The last time I saw Ray was in the early '90s. By then, he had met Jerry and our son, Oliver. "What a nice guy," Jerry said.

We met for lunch in Manhattan at the West Bank Café.

Ray's idea. It would be goodbye. "I need to leave New York, go home to live with my parents in Pennsylvania," he said.

    I nodded, taking in how thin his still handsome face was. Like so many gay men during that era, especially in the theater, Ray was dying of AIDS. Sitting across the table from him, I did more listening than talking as he told me about the myriad ways in which his body had betrayed him.

    Then he said, "I want you to know, you were the last woman I ever loved. I realized if I couldn't be with you, I had to be my true self. Thank you."

    I was dumbstruck. How could he be thanking *me*? "I loved you too," I said. "I love you still."

    We smiled at each other, though there was nothing to smile about, and then, in unison, as if on cue, looked out the window at the marquees of 42nd Street's newly designated Theatre Row, where I would one day perform a few long blocks from Broadway, and where he would not, could not, be again.

8.

After Dallas, I returned to my childhood home in suburban Washington, D.C. for the first extended period since I had left for Interlochen at sixteen. Now twenty-two, without means to support myself, I had no choice. I was lucky. Not everyone had a family who could take them in. Still, coming home deflated me. With a European bus and truck theater tour, two seasons of summer stock, two degrees, and a summer diploma from the Central School of Speech and Drama in London on my resumé, living with my parents felt like a defeat before I'd even gotten started, and a regression—one that I rebelled against at every opportunity. During my actual adolescence, I had cooperated, acted the model teenager, delaying the separation phase that most young people go through in high school until I finished grad school. The fight over Ray's letters started a cold war with my father. He and I didn't speak for the entire year I spent at home. We tiptoed around each other in our small house, maintaining what distance we could by using my mother and sixteen-year-old sister as buffers. Our standoff sucked the life out of our home.

To escape the oppressive atmosphere and to begin my career, I worked three part-time jobs. I taught Shakespeare at the tiny Actors' Stage Studio, a D.C. version of the famous HB Studio in New York. I'm not sure how the director of the school justified my salary—there were only two students in the class—but I'm glad she did. One of the women taking the course became a lifelong friend. The second job offered more prestige and more chaos. The Smithsonian Institution hired me to teach creative dramatics to a huge group of three and four-year-olds. Thirty shrieking children circled me in the lobby, and I lost my trained voice every Saturday morning, as I tried in vain to wrangle them into submission. Though the job was little more than glorified babysitting, the credit sounded substantial. The third job involved office work for Archaesus Productions—an award-winning children's theater company. My officemate was a handsome D.C. actor named Cotter Smith, who went on to a solid acting career on stage, film, and television. Archaesus made me liaison for their special programs. I traveled around the Washington, D.C. area, evaluating facilities for young people with mental, emotional, or physical challenges and made recommendations as to what kind of work the company should present.

I saved every penny, but the sum-total of these gigs didn't add up to a living. I couldn't move out. After dinner I'd hide in my room, which was in fact my brother's room. For years my sister and I had shared a small bedroom, barely big enough to hold two twin beds and two dressers, but she was a teenager now, and I had been used to living alone. There was no way we could room together. We didn't get along as it was. My minor rebellions—gay boyfriend, the cold war with Daddy—scared her.

A few evenings a week, I hung out with a fledgling group of young theater geeks, who had just formed Washington's New Playwrights' Theatre. The guy at the helm had enormous energy and smarts and recognized that I had what it took to run their new play readings, but since I wanted paid work and he wanted my parents as patrons, our agendas didn't align. After baking dozens of chocolate chip cookies for a theater fund-raiser—a sexist assignment for sure—I realized that he'd never give me any real power. Soon after, I left.

My year in limbo included a particularly odd job. The father of one of my Vassar friends, a doctor, hired me to pretend to be a patient so that his med students could work on their diagnostic skills. The doctor assigned me a condition: hyperthyroidism. I studied the symptoms—nervousness, sweating, bulging eyes, rapid speech—and did my best to mimic the complaint when the student doctor questioned me. My biggest challenge was faking a rapid pulse. I worked myself up by running around the medical building beforehand. My "performance" was a big hit and was recorded for future use, but I found the exercise creepy. It was one thing to believe you are a character for the time you spend on stage in that role; it was quite another to apply those skills to life, without your audience knowing it.

Today the job of standardized patient, or SP, has itself been standardized. The organization C3NY supplies SPs to medical programs in the New York City area. The managing director is a former actress of my generation. She considers the job a good way for actors to supplement their incomes and to practice their craft.

Seventeen years after my one SP gig, I was diagnosed with Grave's disease, a form of hyperthyroidism. My friend's father saw something in me, and I'm not referring to talent.

Six months into my post-graduate year, I faced the fact that I wasn't going to make a living in Washington, D.C at a job related to my training. I had to get out, and teaching was my ticket. Armed with my MFA and determined to move my life forward, I applied for entry-level teaching jobs in universities all over the country. Then I waited.

I had a few dates to pass the time: a college friend and I went to an Ivy League alumni mixer and a Harvard guy asked for my number. He picked me up in his sports car, expected me to pay for my dinner, played the piano back at my parent's house, then grabbed me at the door for a pushy, messy kiss. When he called again the next day, I put him off—way too arrogant.

An actor who was playing Aaron Burr to my Theodosia, his daughter, as part of an Actors' Stage Studio new play reading, asked me out. The director thought I was perfect for the period role. "Mr. Burr" was short, mustached, and at least twice my age. When he called to invite to see the Bicentennial fireworks on the Mall, I demurred.

By that time, I was already halfway out the door. I had spent two days in Austin interviewing with the faculty and giving a demonstration class in voice and diction to U.T. students. While waiting for a decision from Austin, and loath to accept the offers from the University of Alabama, the University of Idaho, or the University of Alaska, whose locations seemed more foreign and impossible than the Lone Star, I did something I'd vowed never to do.

With my father grumbling about why I didn't just go get a job, any job, I waited tables at a suburban Maryland restaurant and lasted one day. I took night classes in shorthand and typing—I could type, but not fast enough for a secretarial job. The teacher noticed that I excelled in shorthand and that I had a college degree. She wanted to recommend me to work at the World Bank, suggesting that I leave my MFA and my Phi Beta Kappa status off my resumé. "You'll be perceived as over-qualified," she said.

The disconnect between what I had been trained for, what I had spent my whole life dreaming of, and the reality of working in banking, shook me to my core. *Who was I?* While in the middle of this identity crisis, and about to give in to the only credible living before me, I got the call from the University of Texas Drama Department Chair—an offer of a full-time tenure track instructor position, with a three-year contract. The timing couldn't have been better. He told me that the decision had been unanimous, though there were a couple of assistant professors (men) who worried that I was too young, too close in age to handle the students. I dropped out of shorthand class, hung up my waitressing apron, and didn't look back.

In the car on the way to Dulles Airport to start my new life in Austin, I looked over at my father. He kept his eyes on the road. Never one to make small talk nor to acknowledge the emotional elephant in the room or, in this case, the vehicle, he drove on in silence. Our mutual pain at the terrible rift between us hung in the air. At the airline counter, inside the building, we still couldn't look at each other, only up at the soaring lines of Dulles's glass and beams, but once I had my ticket in hand, at the gate, the realization that we were about to part sunk in. We smiled, weak, sheepish smiles, filled with embarrassment, apology, and love. We hugged and I inhaled my father's familiar spicy aftershave. How I had missed that scent. Daddy. For all the anger and hurt of the past year—Ray, the suggestion that I go on welfare, the wordless months—I was and would always be Daddy's girl. I kissed his cheek. "I love you, Daddy."

He kissed my forehead, as he had every night of my childhood. "And I love you."

Then I walked down the airline breezeway to adulthood.

9.

On my back amidst a sea of AstroTurf green shag carpet, staring up at the popcorn ceiling of a temporary apartment in Austin, my mouth dried up with fear. *What had I done moving back to Texas?* Although I had spent six years, from my senior year in high school until I finished grad school at twenty-two, away from home, traveling the world—Michigan, Switzerland, Italy, France, Greece, Poughkeepsie, Cape Cod, Dallas—homesickness overcame me, as if for the very first time. I grabbed the phone on the floor. The apartment had no furniture, except a mattress.

Three days before, I had arrived in Austin for my first full-time teaching job, and just as I did when I landed in Dallas and headed to the Theater Center, I went straight to the U.T. drama department office to check in and to figure out where to go next. They had arranged for me to stay in a motel until I got settled, but it was sleazy and depressing. I needed a car right away; you couldn't survive in Austin without one, though as a grad student in Dallas I'd managed. I picked out a cute Ford Pinto—the one later recalled, because it could explode—and went to see the realtor recommended by the department. Another new faculty member came too, a very proper middle-aged Englishman, there for a special lectureship. We introduced ourselves and decided in unison to rent apartments in the same complex south of campus. It had a swimming pool, and every unit had an outdoor space—a balcony or a patio. I couldn't wait to get out of the motel and to settle into my new home.

I had needed a furnished apartment on the second floor—the complex had only garden or upstairs choices. After the college incident with Tom, my parents insisted that I rent a second-floor place, though all the apartments had easy access through the front door. If someone wanted to break in, they could. I liked the top floor better anyway. Garden apartments had fenced patios without views, but from the six by eight balcony of an upstairs unit, I could see the sunset. The furniture wouldn't be delivered for a couple of days, so the management put me in this empty green apartment.

"Mom?" Still on my back, I cried into the phone. "I don't know anyone here. I miss you so much. And Daddy." I must have sounded like a five-year-old. For all my travels, I had no real experience of adult life. Or maybe the year I spent at home had erased whatever tentative maturity I had gained on my own. No matter the reason, in that ugly apartment, clinging to the phone, the cord pulled taut from its station on the kitchen wall,

I sank into the reality that for the first time I would be supporting myself, that nothing I'd achieved before this counted the way paying my own bills and doing my own taxes would. I might as well have been a baby learning to walk.

Mother calmed me down, reminding me that once I was in my real place, with all the furniture, I wouldn't feel so lost or lonely. She was right. When I turned the key on my first apartment, the sight made me very happy. The carpet was beige—thank God—still shag, but I could live with it. The couches and chairs sported striped neutral shades of cream and brown. Not my colors, but ones I could work with. And the view of sun and sky freed something inside me.

Once my stuff arrived, I set about putting my stamp on the place: throw rugs and pillows, posters and photos on the walls, a blue and purple Indian bedspread in my ample bedroom on my queen-sized bed, and of course, clothes in the walk-in closet. I loved the gigantic mirror in the vanity area outside the bathroom. Its perimeter of light bulbs reminded me of dressing room lights backstage. I was especially proud of the ceiling to floor wall mural I'd made of dozens of *New Yorker* covers for my dining alcove. I'd read the magazine since my senior year in high school—my subscription followed me to college and grad school and then to Austin. The cover wall represented my intellectual and artistic roots. When I finished it, the generic apartment transformed into home. It was mine.

Once classes started at the university, my sense of rootlessness abated. I threw myself into the job: sixteen classes a week of voice and diction for actors, 9 a.m. until 1 p.m., Monday through Thursday, with office hours in the afternoons. Even with the traffic on Interstate 35, I made it home every day by 4:30. My students were all undergraduate drama majors required to take my course, and no matter how much energy I expended trying to turn vowel formation and vocal resonance into something interesting, I had to acknowledge that this was dull stuff, and for me, too easy. After six weeks, I needed more than speech exercises to occupy my mind and to temper my increasing frustration at not acting.

Thus, I began writing, at first only on Sunday mornings. After eating my breakfast, I would place my trusted Olivetti typewriter on my dining table—the machine had gotten me through college and a graduate thesis—stared up at Eustace Tilly, and with the Texas sun shining through the window behind me, tapped out a play about the poet I'd long been obsessed with: Edna St. Vincent Millay.

One-person shows weren't common in the mid-1970's—only Hal Holbrook as Mark Twain and Julie Harris as Emily Dickinson had made their mark and they were stars. But doing *Happy Days* convinced me that I had what it took to carry one as an actress. I wasn't so sure that I could write one, however, but page by page the play took shape, until two years later, I had a complete script entitled *The Phrase in Air*. In 1978 KUT FM, the University's public radio station, interviewed me and let me do an excerpt. So began an eighteen-year stretch of solo performing.

With Denise, my director, a grad student a few years my senior, I continued to rehearse and rewrite, until we were ready to test the play in front of an audience. With her russet hair, freckles, and sparrow body, Denise resembled the poet more than I did. My connection to Millay was a long-standing passion for her work and deep interest in her life in the arts, which led me to the poet's alma mater, Vassar, where Millay had done theater. Denise had heard that the MacDonald Observatory, which was affiliated with U.T., was looking for people willing to fly to the remote location to "entertain." The handful of astronomers and staff were desperate for distraction. When we proposed bringing the show to them, they said an immediate, enthusiastic, "Yes," offering all expenses paid plus a small honorarium.

Denise suffered from extreme motion sickness and could barely get through the flight on the tiny four-seater plane, despite having downed a couple of Dramamines beforehand. She kept her eyes closed the whole time, while I glued myself to the window and the long, empty miles of West Texas land below. I still couldn't quite believe that a bunch of astronomers would be interested in a play about a female poet, albeit a legendary one, let alone pay for the privilege.

That evening, we held a brief rehearsal. We both understood that the minuscule living room where I would perform would dictate everything I did. *Forget blocking, just don't bump into the audience's knees.* The next night I did a bare bones version of the play, cutting sections every time one of the four—or was it five? —members of the audience looked away or shifted in his seat.

There weren't any women in attendance, except Denise. It felt like a literary version of stand-up comedy, in which the material changed depending on the audience response. In this case, I recited "Renascence," the epic poem that introduced Millay to the world: *All I could see from where I stood/ Was three long mountains and a wood;* and her love sonnets: *I shall forget you presently, my dear, So make the most of this, your little day.*

The assembled seemed grateful and we segued without pause from applause to questions about how I had come to write the play and how Denise and I had worked together. They thanked us for our willingness to fly the long way west to give them an experience other than stargazing.

The next morning at dawn, before our flight back, Denise and I rose to watch the sunrise. She puffed on a cigarette, as one car, miles below us, crossed on the single road, its headlights the only point of focus, like a speeding firefly. Then came a hazy yellow light on the horizon, building up and up until the glow grew too bright to look at, and the sky turned from black to grey to a thin translucent blue. Although I had spent four years in Texas, I hadn't grasped the meaning of "big sky country" until that moment.

It still amazes me that the booking happened at all. When I first moved to the Hudson Valley in 2013, in my new home, unpacking box after box, I would listen to the local NPR radio station, WAMC, something I found soothing no matter the nature of the news. Most of the segments were familiar. They carried *All Things*

Considered and *Weekend Edition, Market Place Money,* and *Fresh Air,* just like WNYC. I discovered the 9 a.m. *Roundtable,* local journalists debating the headlines, and was hooked. I couldn't give up the *Brian Lehrer Show,* so I would listen on my computer during lunch.

And then there was *Star Date.* One of the most breathtaking aspects of moving from the New Jersey suburbs to the Hudson Valley was the unfiltered night sky. I hadn't realized how much light pollution canopied my previous home in Montclair. Here the sky was pure and clear, the stars brilliant and close, as if I could reach up and grab one. *Star Date* was a short segment telling the listener what to look for when looking up. But that's not what hit me. As soon as I heard where *Star Date* originated from, "The MacDonald Observatory," I flashed back to the vast pitch-black night, more epic than the nights here, starker in its treeless, endless vista, and the unique West Texas locale where I had premiered *The Phrase in Air* thirty-five years earlier.

Now, at night in my Red Hook home, I look up, picking out the Big and Little Dippers, the North Star, the Milky Way. In the morning, when I turn on the radio and hear *Star Date,* I think fondly of the gentlemen, many of whom may be gone, who allowed me to try out my first play in their observatory living room—an intimate experience enlarged by our collective awareness of how close to the heavens we were.

I grew up a lot in Austin. I supported myself for the first time and momentously, fell in love with a magnetic young man, a student—he was twenty, I, twenty-four. It was a passionate, tortured affair that blew up my blocks, emotional and sexual, resulting in a case of cystic acne—the external manifestation of the adolescent I still was—and cemented the realization that I, not my parents, had agency over my body and my desires. I could act on them and survive.

"You'll be great at sixty," my insightful-beyond-his-years lover said one day, apropos of nothing. I've thought of his pronouncement many times, especially through my rocky forties and fifties. He saw me whole—present and future—and gave me a marker to look forward to, for which I'm grateful.

Two years into my time in Austin, I turned down a job offer from Virginia Polytechnic Institute in Blacksburg (now Virginia Tech). They had an innovative drama department and loved my creative approach to voice and movement. The position would have been a promotion and a fast track to tenure by age thirty, but it didn't feel right. I couldn't imagine living there, more isolated than I had been in Austin, and I no longer wanted a life in academia—too cloistered—but I simply hadn't been ready socially or emotionally to storm the Big Apple, to go after my dream. I knew that this had to change, so I devised a plan, and as sometimes happens, the plan synchronized with opportunity.

A student designer, who had been moonlighting in the costume shop at the Austin Dinner Theater, told me that they needed to hire a local actress willing to join Actors' Equity Association—the professional union—for a walk-on role in their production of *Goodbye Charlie* with Ruta Lee, a D-list actress from the old Studio system. I vaguely remembered her from the Hollywood musical *Seven Brides for Seven Brothers. Willing?* I jumped at it.

The audition consisted of my one short scene, which opened the show, and required a lot of loud crying. No problem. I was nothing if not loud. And confident. I knew that I could cold read a script, any script. I threw myself onto the imaginary casket of my husband, the title character, and wailed.

"Good lungs. I'm impressed," said the theater director. Then he grilled me about my future intentions. "Are you really moving to New York? It's got to be L.A or New York. I won't give an Equity card to someone staying in Texas." He went on to tell me that there wasn't enough work there, and once you joined the union, you couldn't work in non-union shows. I assured him that I was serious, that I'd quit my job to pursue my acting career. He nodded, convinced, and gave me the part.

Ruta was old-school MGM, complete with a helmet of bouffant blond hair and ridiculously long false eyelashes. She didn't speak to me much. Hadn't even come to rehearsal. She'd been doing this show on the dinner theater circuit for months. When she did address me, it was only to say, "You have pretty eyes. You should accentuate them with lashes." Eager to oblige, I wore them for the length of the run, then never again. I loved lipstick, eyeshadow, and mascara, but hated the weight of artificial lashes, like an awning on my lids.

My casting in that role seems prescient now, widow

that I am. I can't help but believe that I projected not only my character into those I played—starting with Lady Precious Stream—but also my future self (the one my Austin boyfriend had seen so clearly). Regardless, I was happy to have checked "join the Union" off my to-do list. I was ready. Next stop: New York City.

Ambition

An ardent desire for rank, fame, or power; aspiration; may suggest equally a praiseworthy or an inordinate desire

10.

When an emeritus professor at the University of Texas at Austin, an elderly man who had mentored me through my first full-time teaching job, attended *The Phrase in Air*, he responded by saying, "You are ambitious." He knew I had resigned my job and was headed for the Big Apple. I took it as a compliment. Now I see the distinction he made between a cloistered life in academia and the riskier one in show business. He had published books, including a seminal volume on directing, and was highly respected by colleagues across the country, but like many in the university world, he looked down on those outside it. He didn't think ambition was a good thing. He knew what he was looking at. I was, indeed, ambitious, and wanted nothing more than to work on Broadway—every actor's dream.

The closest I got to that goal was on my very first audition in New York City. I was twenty-six and had just arrived from Texas, armed with my newly minted Actors' Equity Card. The card meant a lot to me; it meant that that I belonged in the professional theater world, that I was worthy.

When I first arrived in New York, I stayed in my college roommate's Staten Island apartment. She was away and was generous enough to let me crash there until I found my own place. I didn't waste a minute. Even without a permanent address, I had my headshot and resumés duplicated, bought the trade papers—*Backstage* and *Show Business Weekly*—and started going to auditions. Every day I got on the Staten Island Ferry and headed to Manhattan.

In that first week I went to an open audition, a "cattle call" for the Broadway version of the cult movie *Harold and Maude*, which had starred an elderly but still feisty Ruth Gordon in a weird romance with a teen-aged Bud Cort. The play had roles for young women, who could not connect with morbid-beyond-his-years Harold. The open call wasn't an audition; it was an interview. The casting director took note of my training and my height—in this case, a plus. He also seemed pleased that my baby face could pass for sixteen. It was cheaper to have an adult playing a teen than an underage actor who had to have a minder, a tutor, and restricted rehearsal hours. After the minute-long interview, I left the building and forgot about it.

I was shocked when two days later, the casting director called the apartment. I hadn't had time yet to get an answering service, a point he was touchy about. "I don't usually call actors directly," he said. But he really wanted me to come in to read for the producers. *What?*

"Sure," I said. Next thing I knew I was reading sides—scene pages—along with other young-looking, short actresses in the hallway of a rehearsal room. I was disoriented and petrified. The casting director gave me a nod, and I began to fumble the invisible glass that a production assistant, reading Harold's part, had given me. I must have dropped it, because both he and the casting guy looked away, embarrassed for me. They let me try the scene twice, disastrous both times. My grad school mime training had deserted me. The producers barely looked up from the table.

I didn't know it at the time, but that was, indeed, the closest I would ever get to being cast in a Broadway play. It was little comfort that, a few months later, the show, starring the first actress ever to win an Oscar—silent film star Janet Gaynor—flopped, closing after only four performances. I realize that even had I somehow landed the part, it probably wouldn't have propelled my career. I do believe, however, that I would have at least gotten an agent, some invaluable experience, and an undeniable professional credential. As it turned out, I got a story to tell instead.

After the *Harold and Maude* debacle, I continued to trudge my way through open call after open call, mostly to acclimate myself to what auditioning in the professional theater world required. Even after experiencing a casting session in which I was in the running for a Broadway role, I shifted to the widely held cynical view that shows holding open auditions were already pre-cast. I understood that such fatalism flew in the face of the many hours I spent commuting from my studio apartment on 15th Street and Third Avenue and the midtown call venue. *Why was I making such an effort if it was all for naught?* Like so many other actors, I thought I could beat the odds, be the exception. I'd been given a chance once and would surely be given another someday soon.

When this didn't occur, another need surfaced, the need to express my vision as a writer and performer. Early in my first year in New York, I realized that if I wanted to act, I would have to do what I had done in Austin—write my own material. I wanted to show the world who I could be, to display my wares. I had *The Phrase in Air* ready to go and got it booked into a second-floor walk-up building in the Theater District, but I needed to show my comic side as well.

Just as I arrived in Manhattan from Austin, Texas Chic swept the city. With the advent of the television drama *Dallas*—a huge hit—all things Lone Star became fashionable. *What better subject for my next one-person show?* In no time, I wrote a one-act solo, a gentle satire of the trendy infatuation with Texas, with a big dose of '70s feminism thrown in, entitled *Intensity Jane in New York*, a fictionalized take on my transition from the Lone Star State to New York City.

> *Size is what counts in Texas…That's why I left. So, what am I doin' here? Well, ever since I found out that Texas was a state and not a country, I've wanted to live in New York City; figured it was the only other place in the world where you could live out a tall tale and get*

away with it.

I wore a 10-gallon hat with a large yellow silk rose, a black cowgirl shirt with embroidered yellow flowers, black culottes, and authentic tooled cowboy boots that I brought from Austin. Astride Stud (my childhood hobbyhorse with a sock face and its own cowboy hat), spouting diatribes on anti-female double-standards, and armed with a bottle of *Eau de Skunk* in my holster—Manhattan had its dangers in 1979—I galloped onto whatever Off-Off Broadway stages I could find.

To maximize my performance possibilities, I decided to break into the comedy club scene. One May evening, I went to the open mic night at a club on the Upper Eastside—the Comic Strip—and did a five-minute excerpt from the play. I got a few laughs but left without any assurance that the management would book me.

Outside, close to midnight, I couldn't hail a cab, so I darted under the bus stop shelter across the street to avoid the rain and wait for a ride down 2nd Avenue. A few minutes later, a cute young man wearing a yellow slicker walked up to me and asked, "Been waiting long?" I was in costume. He was undeterred. The bus trip was all it took for us to be smitten. Since we didn't exchange last names—only first ones—(his was Jerry), or phone numbers, I despaired the next day when, attempting to follow the few clues he'd left me, I came up empty. Ten minutes later he called. Jerry had asked the Comic Strip for the cowgirl's number, and they gave it to him—something that would never happen today. He told me that if he hadn't gotten it, he would have shown up at my Quaigh Theater booking. Two weeks after our first date, I knew he was the one. Jerry didn't have to ambush me at the theater; he came as my boyfriend.

The Quaigh Theater was an Off-Off Broadway venue on West 43rd Street. The management gave me a late-night slot to perform the entire one-act, not just the few minutes comedy clubs permitted. It was a relief to be able to do my thing unimpeded and to do so in an atmosphere I understood. The Quaigh's stage, though small, suited my work perfectly. The audience sat above me in mini-amphitheater style. I was on my game, with tons of energy and dead-on timing, charged up by Jerry's presence. It would be the first time he'd see me perform and I did not want to disappoint. Everyone laughed throughout. I felt triumphant.

After the show, Jerry came backstage with two people he didn't know, who had told him that they had to meet me. The man beamed; he was wearing a white suit and white hat. I wondered if he was also a performer. The woman, taller than he, was slender, and more conservatively dressed. They introduced themselves as Roger and Jen and proceeded to tell me how talented I was.

"You are a star, and we want to manage you," Roger said.

What? The sudden, unexpected interest blindsided and flattered me. I knew about agents, but very little about managers. Jerry looked proud, happy for me, and somewhat perplexed. Neither of us knew what to do next. I thanked them, and said I'd be interested in hearing more about what their representation would entail. Then I shook their hands, and Jen handed me a business card. We made plans to meet at a gallery showing of Roger's work in Brooklyn later that month. My radar went off. *He was an artist too?* Still, nothing like this had happened in the two years I'd been knocking around the city, and I owed it to myself to play out their offer.

What if Roger and Jen were the break I'd been looking for?

Jerry insisted on accompanying me to the gallery, located in a dicey section of Brooklyn. We were both pleasantly surprised to find that Roger's artwork was original and impressive, but I still didn't quite know what to make of these two.

Over an outdoor lunch in mid-town Manhattan, Jen spelled out the terms of their management, passing me a copy of their standard contract: 20% of any booking they secured for me, as well as any booking I got for myself while under their management. She painted a picture of national tours and huge venues. I told her that Jerry and I had just gotten together and that I didn't want to travel that much yet.

"Men can get in the way," she warned. "They can be threatened by your success. You might have to choose."

I was taken aback. She seemed to be suggesting that I dump my new boyfriend, which I was not going to do.

Then she said that they could land me an agent for theater, film, and television, as well as comedy. I started to calculate the multiple fees—15% to the agent, 20% to the managers—and wondered how I would make any money. I had other questions too. *How long had they been* managers? Who else did they manage? What work had they gotten those clients? Could I speak to those actors and comedians as references? And why didn't they have an office? I didn't ask the last question, but it bothered me. In the '80s, unlike today, when many reputable agents and managers work from home, even the most marginal professionals had an office.

Jen hedged, "We'll talk more soon," assuring me that she would put me in touch with some clients and that I should look over the contract.

When I got home and began to read, I realized that she had neglected to inform me of the most alarming fact: not only would she and Roger get a cut of whatever I earned for the contract's five-year term, but for anything I made *for the rest of my career life*. No way. This was a red flag, and a deal breaker. I called her and said that I couldn't sign the contract as is and made another proposal. "Could we limit the agreement to one year, see how things go, and exclude the in-perpetuity clause for now?"

"I'm sorry," Jen said. "That's not how we work. If we lay the groundwork for making you a success, we deserve to be paid for whatever that success leads to."

Yikes. I was both disappointed and relieved. The whole thing felt too good to be true. She hadn't given me references or answered my questions about their management history. *Who were these people? Parasites? Pretenders?* I couldn't wait around to find out.

"You dodged a bullet," Jerry said. To his credit, he stepped in and proceeded to take on the multiple roles of unpaid manager-publicist-groupie-prop person-bodyguard. The last was no joke. Some of the clubs I performed in that year made seedy look respectable. Together we hit the big-name ones: the famed Improv, whose manager invited me back; Catch a Rising Star, where Richard Belzer was master-of-ceremonies; the Lone Star Café, the epitome of New York Texas Chic, but rowdier than I could handle; and Folk City of Bob Dylan fame.

At the Swiss Chalet on Long Island, where I opened for a faux Texas band, I was booed off the stage without getting to sing my wry version of "The Yellow Rose of Texas." On the way home, my head on Jerry's shoulder, I decided I'd had enough. The club scene, with its late nights and drunken patrons, wasn't for me. A year had proven as much. I was an actress. I needed an audience that would listen and not dismiss me out of hand. I needed to work in theaters.

Because *Intensity Jane in New York* was a one-act, I decided to write a companion piece to fill a full theatrical evening. During the same time that I was making the rounds of comedy clubs, I had landed a gig as a look-alike for Queen Elizabeth II. Her Royal Highness was twenty-five years older than me, but the owner of the celebrity look-alike agency thought my resemblance to the young queen on Britain's stamps was good enough. I appeared along with other look-alikes—Madonna, Pee-Wee Herman, Robert DeNiro, Cher—at parties and in street fairs. Why not make the character the subject of a play? Another satire was born: *The Queen's in the Kitchen*. The premise was simple. *What if the staff at Buckingham Palace went on strike and the Queen had to make her own toast?*

I found a powder blue satin ball gown and long white gloves at a vintage clothing store in Greenwich Village, took a navy-blue silk scarf and fashioned a sash, bought a tiara from a costume shop, and perfected my British accent with the help of dialect tapes and my experience playing Englishwomen in school and summer stock.

> *I am frequently asked to explain the proper form for a wave. Simple really. Raise your arm... Everyone together now! That's right, so that the elbow is in line with the shoulder; curl the fingers ever so slightly; now slowly rotate the wrist a quarter turn—that's it—while moving the arm back and forth as if in slow motion. That way you appear to be waving to people on both sides of the avenue without straining your arm. This should be extremely useful to those of you who expect to ride in a motorcade.* (rubbing her arm) *"Queen's elbow."*

And so, I segued from a world where I didn't belong back to the world in which I was most comfortable. I have no regrets about the time I spent in comedy clubs. I needed a place to tryout my original characters and the clubs provided one.

Best of all, my flirtation with comedy brought me a lasting love. If I hadn't gone to the Comic Strip that fateful night in 1981, I wouldn't have met my husband; I wouldn't have my son. Two and a half years after our encounter at the bus stop at 82nd and Second Avenue, we got married there to what would now be considered viral media attention from all the local TV stations and news services. When we rented a city bus to take us to our reception at the Rainbow Room in Rockefeller Center, the Port Authority publicized the wedding. My mother refused to attend "a wedding on the street," so neither of my parents came, but in a kind of cosmic balancing, the world showed up for us. I have hundreds of clippings from all over the world about our quirky "I dos."

I immediately understood the irony that my fifteen minutes of fame had come not from my life in the theater, but from love.

Failure

A lack of success, a falling short; deficiency; one that has failed

11.

While visiting my parents' home for the weekend with my brother, I did something I had never done in front of my family: reveal doubts about my future. I don't remember how the conversation started, but I do remember my garrulous mother falling silent, my father staring at me, and my brother George, in shock, looking at the floor of the living room. My mother's large abstract watercolors with their bold hues and strong, confident brushstrokes covered the walls; she was at her most brave in her work. She filled the room's built-in shelves with books and with folk toys from around the world and every inch of floor space with mid-century modern furniture. Into this tasteful but crowded setting, I dropped my bombshell.

"I'm quitting theater."

And bombshell it was. As the eldest of three bright, talented children—my brother was the middle child, my sister the youngest—a lot had been expected of me.

Failure was not an option. Education and achievement trumped all in our family. Unlike many more conforming parents, mine supported my ambition to become an actress. They loved the theater and had season tickets to every pre-Broadway show at Washington, D.C.'s National Theater from the late '50s through the '70s.

As a little girl, I stayed awake, waiting for them to come home with tales of legend after legend: Alfred Lunt and Lynn Fontanne's last show together, *The Visit*, Judy Holliday in *Bells Are Ringing*, Zero Mostel in *A Funny Thing Happened on the Way to the Forum*, and Carol Channing in *Hello, Dolly!* I'd sit on the staircase in my pajamas and drink in my mother's pronouncements. She declared Holliday a star and Channing one of a kind, but it was tales of Lunt and Fontanne, the greatest acting team in theater history, which inspired me the most. I dreamed that one day, maybe I, too, would meet and marry an actor and spend our life touring together, in sync on stage and off.

When I was ten years old, as a special treat, my father took me to see *Carnival!* with Jerry Orbach, Anna Maria Alberghetti, and Kay Ballard. We sat in the National's front row. Orbach's puppet scene and Alberghetti's pure rendition of "Love Makes the World Go 'Round" enchanted me, and the sharp comic energy of Ballard's "Always, Always You" was electric. Ballard played the incomparable Rosalie. The character name felt like a sign.

Ethel Merman's revival of *Annie Get Your Gun* in 1966 left me with the impression that she didn't act so much as exert her mesmerizing will. Later I saw the indomitable Pearl Bailey in a revival of *Hello, Dolly!* and the next year, Julie Harris in *Forty Carats*, and Orbach, for a second time, in *Promises, Promises*. Though I wasn't much of a singer, those musicals sealed my love of the stage, and their stars spoke to my sense of destiny. I had to be up there. Somehow.

My parents preferred straight plays, and though the content was often over my head, they didn't hesitate to share their impressions of Archibald MacLeish's *J.B.* with Christopher Plummer, Geraldine Page in *Sweet Bird of Youth*, Eartha Kitt in *The Owl and the Pussycat*, and Margaret O'Brien, who I remembered as a child actor in the film *Meet Me in St. Louis*, all grown-up in *A Thousand Clowns*. I was only seven when they took me to see *Sunrise at Campobello* with Ralph Bellamy playing F.D.R. I didn't understand the drama's political backdrop, but the story's emotional power—the tragedy of a man stricken with a crippling illness and his triumph over it—held me. I wanted to be part of that power. By the time, my father and mother gave their reviews of Jessica Tandy in Edward Albee's *A Delicate Balance*, I was a teenager, babysitting my siblings, and completely determined to have a life in the theater.

Was it my parent's, especially my mother's, high regard for acting royalty that gave my aspirations legitimacy? In part, yes. It was also an in-born longing to express myself in exactly this form. Ours wasn't a religiously observant family, so the spiritual vacuum left by our secular upbringing was filled for me by the magic, mystery, and ritual of the theater. The stage became a sacred space where I could feel a deep human and divine connection.

Fast forward to this humiliating confession. I was in my late twenties and had been in New York for over 2 years. Not much had come of it: a bunch of auditions, some voice-over work, and part-time teaching at the American Musical and Dramatic Academy, the New School, and the Sonia Moore Studio—not much besides one major exception—meeting the love of my life at a bus stop. But career-wise, I felt lost and humbled. So rather than do what I usually did around my parents—talk up the good stuff, i.e., the two new shows, the audition callbacks, the *almosts* —I leveled with them.

"I'm not making it. I've tried, but it's not working and it's time to cut my losses." As the words came out of my mouth, my chest and throat filled with shame like a thick syrup, too rich to digest.

"What will you do?" My father asked quietly. He was always quiet. There was no condemnation, but also no encouragement. He chose his words carefully. Ever the attorney.

"I'm not sure." True. I hadn't thought beyond the admission. Then, before I knew what I was saying, "I'm thinking of going to law school."

My father's eyes grew wide. This had been his dream, that one of his children would follow him into the profession he loved. My brother had been the chosen one. George and Daddy had had a huge fight when my brother declared that he was going to be a writer and wanted to go to grad school to study poetry. Our father never quite recovered from the disappointment. Now I had given him new hope.

"Really?" he said, begging me to say it again.

"Yes, maybe. I'm a bit old, but—"

"You're not too old," he interjected. "I was about your age when I started law school in this country." Arthur Blooston had gone to law school twice—once in Poland and once at the University of Minnesota, where he and my mother had met.

George looked at me, gobsmacked. He clearly didn't believe me. Mother pursed her lips, skeptical too. They were right. As soon as I said the words "law school," I knew I didn't really mean it. But I didn't take back the statement immediately. I couldn't. The yearning in my father's face stopped me.

"I have to think this through," I said.

George and I retreated to the kitchen, leaving our parents to talk alone. "I couldn't have done that," my brother said.

"Say you are going to law school? Yes, I remember."

"Admit failure," George said. He, too, was struggling with writing jobs for magazines and the limited income they offered.

"It's just too hard to keep putting a happy face on this."

"Law school is incredibly boring." *Was he lobbying me to stay the course?*

"I know." Just moments after blurting out my new plan, after raising my father's hopes more than I could have realized, I was already losing ground. I felt myself sink with the sure knowledge that I couldn't go through with such a radical detour from my true self. I didn't want to be a lawyer, hadn't ever, didn't now. I had spilled the confusion, frustration, and pain, and wondered aloud what could I do, if I couldn't succeed as an actress? I should have talked this through with a friend before exposing my parents to my doubts. My father's feelings were collateral damage. Now I added guilt at jerking him around to my shame at failing.

I don't remember exactly what I said—I'm sure that I fumbled and stuttered—or how long it took me to walk back the idea, but I know that I did so that very weekend. George looked relieved. The reversal surprised no one, least of all, my father. He sighed, nodded, and gave me a little smile, as if he was glad that we had diffused the momentary madness. In a more conforming home, the madness would have been attempting a life in the theater. In my family, the opposite was true. Though they sometimes resisted, as in my brother's case, our parents ultimately recognized their children's essential selves and honored the paths we chose.

After I spoke, my father gently affirmed his belief in my talent, "You will make it. But you might consider that you have all this backwards. Most actors do solo shows once they have established a reputation in the conventional theater." He was thinking of Holbrook and Harris, both of whom he'd seen. He wasn't wrong. At that time, what I was attempting was unusual. Then he kissed me on the forehead, just as he had at the airport after our year of silence. I didn't quite believe him. Already, I knew too much about how show business worked, and my cynicism infected his vote of confidence. I couldn't embrace it. I couldn't buy into the notion he had spouted many times: that the cream always rises to the top. He was convinced that I was the cream. I wasn't so sure. But in this moment of vulnerability, I believed the love.

We never talked about law school again.

12.

Recommitted to making it, I decided to take the Millay show further. I had a problem though, a big one: I didn't have the rights to perform it. The play included a lot of poetry, all of which was controlled by Edna's sister, Norma Millay, her literary executor.

I consulted a respected New York entertainment attorney. She was kind but firm, "You're either going to have a career or you aren't. Don't start it with a lawsuit."

I left her office sure about what I had to do, shaking off the not-so-subtle implication that most actors fail. Never mind. I would stay focused on my immediate goal. I had to persuade Norma Millay that my play was worthy of her endorsement.

Edna's little sister had quite a reputation: cranky and withholding concerning her famous sibling's life and works. She had turned down several authors who wanted to write authorized biographies, as well as playwrights, and screenwriters. *How could I, an unknown young actress, fare any better?*

Norma lived reclusively at Steepletop, Edna's country home in Austerlitz, New York on the Massachusetts border. The house was modest, but the land had a kind of wild grandeur. In 1975, she had transformed the property into the Millay Colony for the Arts. In 1980, I wrote to Norma, and got no response. I needed a personal connection to reach her, so I researched the board members of the Colony. Maybe there was someone I could call on, someone who would help me.

Beatrice Straight, the surprise Oscar winner for her supporting role as the embittered wife of Peter Finch in *Network*, was on the board. One afternoon while attending a play in New York with my mother, I noticed Ms. Straight sitting about three rows behind us, across the aisle. "Why don't you go up to her?" Mom said, the shy woman always pushing me to do what she wouldn't have dared. I turned and looked at the regal lady with the huge blue eyes and pale complexion and thought, *I can't.* But I did and she gave me her card.

When I wrote to her, Miss Straight answered, saying that the actor Roscoe Lee Browne was a more active board member than she and very close to Norma. She gave me his contact information. I knew that Mr. Browne had performed at the Washington Theater Club under Hazel Wentworth, my childhood director—a point of connection, however tenuous.

I wrote all this in a letter and sent a copy of my script. Shortly thereafter, Mr. Browne called me. His deep basso voice and perfect, classical enunciation electrified me and lifted me out of my modest studio apartment. I couldn't believe I was speaking with an actor I so admired. "I'd be happy to introduce you to Miss Millay. We both think the play is really good. She called it 'exquisite,'" Browne said, adding, "I don't know of any actress who would go to the lengths you have gone to in order to create work for herself."

That was then. Now, of course, everyone with a phone is creating a YouTube channel and a show of their own.

With Mr. Browne's introduction, I went to Steepletop. A tiny woman with waist length white hair and a long, sharp nose came out to great us, along with the head of the Colony, a tall, slender, much younger woman. After a bit of small talk, the pivotal moment arrived: I performed, in costume, excerpts of the play for Norma in Edna's living room—a cramped, dark space, with barely any area in which to move. (My MacDonald Observatory experience stood me in good stead.) The experience was surreal. There I was, reciting Millay's poetry, as Edna, for her sister, in their home. Throughout, Norma looked up at me without nodding or giving any sign yea or nay. When I was done, she patted the seat next to her.

"You certainly speak well," she said. "I will give you the rights to use the poetry in your play for educational performances and Off-Off Broadway. Not Off-Broadway or Broadway." I don't know why she withheld her unencumbered permission, but I took what she gave and ran with it.

For the next several years, I paid Norma Millay an 8% royalty on everything I made from *The Phrase in Air*:

on tour to schools, including Vassar, NYC's legendary Players Club, Lincoln Center Library, and Bargemusic on the Brooklyn waterfront, at the National Portrait Gallery in Washington, D.C., where my performance was recorded for Voice of America, and finally, five months pregnant, at the Woodstock Playhouse.

Woodstock marked my final performance of *The Phrase in Air*, and fittingly the best. *The Poughkeepsie Journal* called it "stunning...a revelation. Millay would have been pleased." (It wasn't lost on me that Meryl's rave review as a college student was in the same newspaper.) The play was also the most lucrative of my monologues. By then I had a booking agent, an old friend who had a show on John Keats and who had formed a company, *Living Literature*, securing far more money for his artists than we could have commanded on our own.

And though I gradually let my dreams of Off-Broadway and Broadway go, I had paved the way for other solo performers. Actors' Equity Association created a new contract, the Periodic Performance Agreement, especially for me; it became the standard for Actor-Producers doing their own work. *Backstage Magazine* did a feature on the *Living Literature* group, called, "Create a One-Person Show," for which I was interviewed. I was a pioneer in the solo arena, a real achievement.

When I wrote the play, at all of twenty-six years old, I gave my version of Edna the line, "People are so much more important than poetry is." Norma Millay cashed all the checks I sent, but I never saw or heard from her again, nor from Roscoe Lee Browne, nor from Beatrice

Straight, though I invited them to my performances. Still, it was their assistance and support that allowed *The Phrase in Air* to have the full life it deserved. I am indebted to them.

13.

August 1985. Edinburgh, Scotland. For months I had been planning my week at the renowned Edinburgh Festival. I was slated to perform in its burgeoning Fringe Festival, considered a launching pad for many up-and-coming actors, comedians, and musicians, and would showcase my two one-person comedies, *Intensity Jane in New York*, and its companion piece, *The Queen's in the Kitchen*.

After testing them together at various Off-Off Broadway venues and in interviews on a Manhattan Cable show, I was ready to cross the Atlantic. My husband of less than two years was totally supportive. An advertising copywriter with a great eye, he took hilarious photographs of me in character for posters and pre-publicity: Intensity entering the Downtown E and A subway station, menacing over the shoulder stare, toy gun drawn—something that would never be allowed today—and the Queen, in our Park Slope apartment kitchen, in full regalia wielding a wooden spoon in one hand and a pot cover in the other, eyes wide, caught, as if by paparazzi.

The Fringe gig was all on our dime: from the rental, sight unseen, of the Caledonian Club's stage, to the hotel room, the car, the train from London, and the airplane tickets. *Worth it*, I thought. An investment in my career.

The theater space was disappointing. It wasn't a theater at all, but a basement with a postage stamp stage, no wings, the barest minimum lighting, and no sound system—thank goodness we brought our boom box and cassette tapes. *What could I do?* Cope. That's what professionals did, and I was nothing if not professional. Jerry acted as my stage manager, house manager, and box office ticket taker. We were a team.

In the few days leading up to my opening I heard that Eric Bogosian, a solo performer who had taken the New York theater scene by storm, was playing at The Assembly Rooms. We went to see him and were excited both by the work and by the venue. Excited and envious. This was where I wanted to be. The Assembly Rooms stood in for Off Broadway against my Off-Off Broadway at the Caledonian Club. Even today, over 30 years later, The Assembly Rooms are a coveted Fringe site. The Caledonian Club no longer exists.

After the show, Jerry had the presence of mind to contact Bogosian's manager to offer the actor a complimentary ticket to my double bill. We crossed our fingers that he would show up.

Meanwhile, I needed to get ready. At my dress rehearsal I met the solo performer who had the venue in the slot immediately before mine. She was a sight: older, probably in her sixties, smeared make-up, feathers in her hair, and babbling non-stop. I told Jerry, "If you ever see me becoming even the slightest version of that woman, make me stop this." He looked at me, bemused, and said nothing. "No, I'm serious. That's a path I can't go down."

My plays opened. The photos, posters, and the glossy brochure that Jerry had designed garnered interviews with *The Scotsman*, the city's main newspaper, and *Radio Forth*, Edinburgh's radio station, as well as three strong reviews:

> "A very entertaining double-bill by a vivacious and obviously talented comedienne" (Radio Forth)
>
> "Amusing, zesty, shoot-from-the-hip-tell-it-like-it-is style" (The Scotsman)
>
> "Both performances are highly professional and together they display Ms. Blooston's versatility and humour." (Festival Times)

The attention also got me a death threat, delivered by hand-written letter to the Caledonian. A Scottish Nationalist took issue with the idea that Elizabeth II was *their* Queen. I didn't talk about Scotland in the play, but the title must have provoked him. "*The* Queen's in the Kitchen." I read the rant, fascinated and shaken, but we decided not to go to the police. "You're getting enough visibility to bring out the kooks," Jerry said proudly.

Audiences were sparse, but I felt, given the critical

kudos, that the five-day run had already been a success. The final performance was a matinee on Bogosian's last day in Edinburgh. He came, along with a producer from Manhattan Punchline, a young New York City theater devoted to comedy, located on Theatre Row. There was only one other person in the audience. I gave it my all. Two out of three of them could change my life.

Crying alone works fine. Laughing takes a group. When that group is miniscule, audience members feel pressured to respond and they freeze. Nevertheless, afterwards, Eric told Jerry that I should call him when I got back to New York, and the Punchline producer said that he'd be happy to book me later that year. I was elated. The giant effort and expense—the crapshoot—had paid off with another paid gig and a bona fide professional contact.

But it was the phone call with Eric Bogosian two weeks after the festival that left the most profound impression from my time in Edinburgh. At home in Brooklyn, sitting on the floor of our bedroom, my legs tucked tightly under me, every muscle coiled, my whole being listening as if my life depended on what this actor, who had revolutionized the art of the monologue, thought of me.

"I couldn't have done what you did. I don't have the discipline," Eric said.

"What do you mean?" I asked.

"Do a show for three people. You're more professional than I would have been. You're too professional for a venue like that." I thought he was complimenting me.

Then he went on. "You need to be seen only in places as professional as you are. Otherwise, you are wasting your time and talent. You need someone to help you do that, an agent or a manager."

I must have mumbled something like, "You're right." The specter of Roger and Jen flitted across my consciousness. *Had I missed my chance?*

Then I told Eric about Manhattan Punchline. He said that was a step in the right direction. I was acutely aware that he wasn't offering his contacts to me, just his advice. I thanked him and felt a slow wave of nausea and humiliation. His succinct assessment of my ongoing predicament tainted the admiration for my abilities that he had expressed. I felt like a loser.

Only a few months before, I had performed the two acts in an Off-Off Broadway theater pretentiously named The New Vic, the only elevated aspect of the place. My dressing room wall had a large hole that blasted the February chill. Its lobby restrooms contained filthy bathrooms; the men's room stank of urine that turned the white tile walls yellow. The day before my plays opened, I put on rubber gloves, kneepads, and a scarf around my nose, and hauled a bucket of Pine Sol into the stinking stalls, got on my hands and knees, and scrubbed it clean.

Jerry came over after work and asked, "What the hell are you doing?"

I sighed, licked the sweat off my upper lip. "I can't have my parents using filthy bathrooms." They would attend the plays that weekend.

Jerry picked up a broom and swept the lobby floor.

Eric had summed up my situation correctly. I *was* too good for this, but I felt powerless to change my trajectory. I heard the echo from Hazel Wentworth's remark almost twenty-five years earlier. "Professional" had become both what I was and wasn't. No matter. I needed to act wherever and whenever I could. That need trumped my standards for professionalism, which only applied to the quality of the work itself and not to the circumstances in which I presented it.

So, I brushed aside his advice. It was too overwhelming, and I was too scared. If I started saying "no" to the venues and offers available to me, I might never act again. If I waited to get an agent or a manager, I might wait forever. The thought of not performing frightened me more than the idea that performing would only count if I did so under the right conditions. I told myself I was making progress: on to the Punchline.

It would take many years and many more marginal performances to understand exactly what Eric had tried to communicate. Meanwhile, he went on to great acclaim on stage, screen, and television. *Talk Radio* was nominated for a Pulitzer Prize. I didn't react as viscerally when I saw his work or heard about his successes as I did when I saw or heard about Meryl's—maybe because he was a man—or maybe because I had begun to recognize the undeniable difference between a real career and one that didn't take off.

Drive

*to carry on or through energetically; to urge relentlessly to continuous exertion;
an urgent, basic, or instinctual need*

14.

Over time, my ambition manifested in constant, forced self-motivation. My brother called me "driven." Drive is the engine revving continuously towards it knows not what. Mine had a relentless dynamism, along with the implied exhaustion, physical as well as psychological. I was happy only when I had a creative project to work on, to look forward to, to challenge me. I didn't recognize myself without one. I was my drive, and my drive was me. It dictated my priorities, both professional and personal.

One evening, about a month after we returned from Edinburgh, a former University of Texas student invited Jerry, me, and my brother, to a party in Brooklyn, not far from where we all lived. The host had failed to tell me that my Austin boyfriend would be there. As soon as he walked in, he made a beeline in my direction and enveloped me in a long hug. Jerry and George were sitting at a table nearby. I could feel two sets of eyes trained on us. The attraction was palpable to everyone. I introduced him and then we moved to an adjacent room to talk privately. The last I'd heard from him was that he, too, had gotten engaged. I remember thinking that he had called to get my permission or blessing or both. Little did I know that he had broken it off. Now our experiences would truly diverge.

Later that night, when Jerry and I got home, the first thing out of his mouth was "Let's have a baby."

I paused, wondering where this was coming from, then asked, "When?"

"Now." Jerry was firm, adamant, and jealous. My husband had never seen me with another man and felt threatened. He wanted to stake his claim and having a child together would do that like nothing else could.

I smiled and took his face in my hands. "Soon. First I have to write this play for Punchline." It sounded lame. I kissed him. "You are my husband. I chose *you*."

The Punchline producer had agreed to let me write a new show for a December production. I had the subject: motherhood. My relationship with my mother was complicated. I loved her, thought the world of her, and was afraid of turning into her, of losing my performer self, if I had a child. That complexity informed *Mad Moms*—my first multi-character solo. I was inspired by Whoopie Goldberg and Lily Tomlin, who had done their own multi-character shows. The play would satirize the perils of this fundamental role: Stage Mom, Shopaholic

Mom, Supermom, the mother of a serial killer, New Age Pregnant Mom, and a little girl, Rosie Ann, who literally blew it all up.

As Rosie Ann's Mom said about her dangerously headstrong progeny, "*I got to give her credit. At least she's expressin' herself.*"

The play practically wrote itself. Three weeks after I began, the script was done. The run at Punchline was a success. Then, on New Year's Eve, I said to Jerry, "Okay. Let's go for it." My demons had been exorcised with comedy. I had faced my fears by creating a vehicle for them, and now, with the project completed, I could shift gears to focus on what we wanted as a couple.

One champagne bottle later, I was pregnant. First try. Timing is everything, as is the "urgent, basic, instinctual" drive to create.

15.

While I made the rounds of New York area theaters trying to land bookings for *Mad Moms*, a publicist, to whom I had been referred, suggested that I contact the Whole Theater in Montclair, New Jersey. It took forty non-rush hour minutes to drive there from Brooklyn, where I lived with my husband and eighteen-month-old son. I thought, sure, it was worth a look.

Spring was the most beautiful time in Montclair. "May in Montclair" became an annual event, attracting city dwellers, who strolled and drove past the cherry trees lining the town's quiet blocks, and the azaleas and lush gardens dressing up Colonials, Tudors, Victorians, and Craftsman mansions. Montclair's shops and restaurants put out pots of impatiens and geraniums to lure customers. The town reminded me—especially its homes and tall oaks—of where I grew up. Jerry and I had been thinking seriously about moving to a place of our own. Like most young couples with children, we had a lot to consider: Jerry's commute to his job in Manhattan, Ollie's schooling, my connection to an arts community, and my need to stay close to the city for auditions and bookings.

But the day I went to Montclair for the first time, I wasn't thinking about a potential move to the suburbs. I wanted the powers-that-be at the Whole Theater to book my show. Those powers were the actress Olympia Dukakis and her brother Apollo. After decades as a respected stage actress, Olympia's film career had taken off. Her performance in *Moonstruck* was the talk of Hollywood. She went on to win an Oscar, thanking her colleagues at the Whole Theater in her acceptance speech.

I didn't get to meet Olympia that day, but I left my polished packet of PR materials with a young woman in the office. I had fallen instantly in love with this gem of a theater, an intimate space with just the right vibe. I desperately wanted to work there. On my way out, I picked up a flyer in the lobby for a new women's writers' group, headed by Olympia, called The Gathering. The group met once a month on a Tuesday evening. Any writer, of any genre, and any level of accomplishment—novice or pro—could join. I had been working on my own for so long that I didn't know how much I yearned for peers and connection, until I read the notice.

The Whole Theater didn't book my show, but the next month I returned to Montclair for my first meeting of The Gathering. It was held upstairs in the theater's green room. As you may or may not know, green rooms are rarely green. This one had beige walls and plain furniture; it was large enough for a big cast to wait when not on stage. Folding chairs formed a circle for the approximately thirty women in attendance: young, middle-aged, old, black, white, large, and small. We sat, smiling at each other with the nervous friendliness that characterized any first encounter. Then in walked the woman who had brought us together.

Olympia was even more impressive in person than on screen: strong, fiercely intelligent, with a loud throaty voice, flashing eyes that bore into you, and a warm, broad smile that softened her chiseled mask-like features. She welcomed us and we proceeded around the circle introducing ourselves and telling a bit about our writing life. The variety of stories struck me, as did the universal desire for community.

One woman, who sat directly across from me, caught and held my attention. She wore shorts and a sleeveless top. Her eyes were ringed with shadows. She looked like she hadn't slept in weeks. When she spoke, despite the obvious fatigue, irrepressible energy filled her voice. She had been a young actress in Los Angeles, done a pilot with Eve Arden and Don Knotts, followed her then boyfriend east, met her husband in a children's theater troupe, married him, moved to Montclair for his job at the local private school, and had two small daughters. Now she worked as a storyteller at children's parties, creating her own solo work. Her name was Shari. I knew right away that we would understand each other.

Then it was my turn. I told the group about my

theater background and solo work. After the introductions, Olympia invited anyone who wanted, to read or perform. Most of the women were poets. A few wrote short stories. One or two were working on memoirs. Unlike Shari and me, they weren't actors. I figured that this was my shot—an audition if you will—for the great Olympia Dukakis. I stood and did a sliver of a monologue from *Mad Moms*. Olympia nodded, eyes wide. She laughed in the right places, as did the others. I left feeling that I had found an important connection.

Over the next few months, I continued to attend the monthly meetings. Sometimes Olympia would be there, sometimes not. During this time, I convinced Jerry to consider moving out of the city. The Park Slope co-ops we could afford didn't have yards. The public schools were fine for grade school, but iffier for middle and high school. He had grown up with a yard, and trees, and flowers, in a small upstate New York town, so when he finally saw Montclair, it resonated with him too. We found a realtor, put in a bid, and in early June 1989, moved from Brooklyn. Going over the bridge for the last time as a city resident, I cried. Ten years of city living—the end of an era.

A few days later, Shari showed up at my door, her little girls in tow. She boldly stated that she needed a friend here, and that as soon as I had walked into The Gathering, she knew I would be one.

"We both have professional acting experience, and intelligence, and we're both mothers. We're connected."

I liked how direct and unguarded she was. We sat among my boxes and talked. "I need your help," she said. She had been tapped by Olympia to direct the next Gathering show. She asked if I would co-direct. Olympia had already given her permission.

Only a month earlier we had both been in a Gathering reading directed by Olympia herself. She had me do the Supermom monologue from *Mad Moms*—an ambition-crazed mother who gave birth while dictating memos. After the performance she looked me in the eye, pointed, and said, "YOU."

Shari had a concept for the next reading, more complex than simply standing and reciting. She wanted to create a sense of cohesion more like a choreographed piece than a recital. I agreed. It was a tall order. We found ourselves training the cast as we went. Few of them knew how to stand on stage, how to project, let alone move and reveal emotion.

The night of the show, a one-night-only affair, we were elated. We had created visual interest by staging the women around the set on the risers and platforms that were already there for the current mainstage production and used music and lighting for transitions between pieces. This was a far cry from the single row of chairs on stage for the previous reading.

Olympia hadn't seen any rehearsals. Usually, she would show up at the dress rehearsal, but she trusted us and must have been busy with bigger projects. We were both eager to demonstrate what we could do. We sat a few rows behind her and noted every twitch from her formidable shoulders.

With a few glitches, and some stiffness from the least experienced poets, the show came off. The audience responded with enthusiastic applause. Shari and I felt triumphant. Until we saw Olympia's face. She turned and marched up the aisle, steaming. She glared at us, and said loudly, well within earshot of the surrounding audience, "WHAT WAS THAT?"

"What do you mean?" I said, running to catch up with her as she stormed out of the theater.

"All that movement. They aren't actors. Stand and speak, that's all they can do."

Shari and I were mortified. We followed her up to the green room for a reception with the cast and their friends and families, a celebration shut down by Olympia's manifest displeasure. My husband, holding Ollie's hand, asked me if I was okay.

"No. The queen is angry."

"Talk to her," he said.

I approached Olympia, who by this time was avoiding Shari and me. I reminded her that she had said we could do whatever we wanted, and we did. We had set out to do something creative, something different.

"Well, you certainly did that," she said, looking me up and down. "But it wasn't appropriate. These women are not professionals like you."

I didn't let the backhanded compliment throw me, loaded as it was given my history. I stood my ground. "I disagree. They pulled it off. It was so much more interesting than an ordinary reading."

"We don't need interesting. Just audible and clear."

I shook my head. "Then why did you want us to

direct them?"

"Because you are experienced performers," she said, with a huff. Then she moved in close to me. By this time, we were in the center of the room. All eyes were on us. "Why are you here anyway?"

"What?"

"I've seen you perform. You're terrific. What are you doing here? You should be in New York, acting."

"I, I just moved here. With my family," I said, nodding towards Jerry and Ollie.

Olympia didn't look at them. She went on, "You're wasting your time here. This is not a professional group, and you can't turn it into one."

Was she kidding? "You're wrong," I shouted. Yes, we were bellowing at each other now. Like family. "I don't understand how you can't see that we gave these writers a worthwhile experience, that the audience loved it, that this is what The Gathering should be doing." I was telling her how to run her group. Oscar-winning Olympia Dukakis. And I was doing it at the top of my lungs.

She matched me roar for roar. "You think you know what this group should be?!"

"YES," I said. I was in the moment and outside it at the same time, locking eyes with Olympia, not backing down. "I certainly do. I don't know what you are worried about. The show was free. It's not as if anyone was asking for their money back."

"Ha. You want to direct? Go into the city and direct. You want to act, the same. Why are you hiding here?"

"Hiding? I just got here! I'm talking to you. I'm arguing with you. This is hardly hiding!"

Olympia smiled—I had scored a point. Then she turned away.

I felt Jerry's hand on my elbow gently pulling me towards the door. One of Jerry's bosses, who had seen me perform in the city a few weeks earlier, asked why he had moved me to the suburbs when I so clearly needed to stay in New York City for my career. Jerry had mumbled that Montclair had been my idea. True. I thought we could all be happy there. I looked over at Shari, who seemed stunned. As I left, everyone stared at the floor.

That night, I cried on the phone to Shari. "How could Olympia have misinterpreted our efforts so completely? How could she not appreciate what we did?"

"You're both very stubborn," Shari said. "We all are."

"Oh my God," I said. "I've ruined my relationship with the most powerful theater person in town and I've just moved here!"

"No, you haven't."

"What do you mean?"

Then Shari told me that after I left Olympia said I was a real "pistol" and would make a great addition to The Gathering's Steering Committee. Shari was already a member. "She was so impressed that you stood up to her. She loved it. You weren't afraid of her. That doesn't happen often. She asked me to invite you on."

I was floored. "Uh. Okay. Thanks."

Olympia, Shari, and I lived on the same street in Montclair—Upper Mountain Avenue, a north-south road that tied the town together. I lived in a tiny one-bathroom Dutch Colonial in Upper Montclair near Montclair State University (then Montclair State College), where I would soon get a job as an adjunct professor in the drama department. Shari lived at the other end of the long street in a house owned by the school her husband worked for. Olympia's house, a classic colonial, high on a hill with a winter view of New York City, sat smack in the middle, equidistant between Shari's and mine. A few weeks later we joined the rest of the Steering Committee in Olympia's kitchen to plan the next year. Not a word from her about what had passed between us, just a warm welcome.

My time on the Steering Committee was brief, not because of conflict, but because, a few months later the Whole Theater folded—less than a year from the time I had moved to town. It struck me as personal bad luck, but of course it had nothing to do with me. The theater had been in financial trouble for a long time and with Olympia's ever-expanding film career, she and her brother didn't have the will to keep it afloat.

I look back on our big fight and picture Olympia and me on the green room "stage," surrounded by writers and strangers, battling about...what? *Who was in charge? Whose vision was correct? Who I was?* That fight, still vivid today, was another moment in which I had been seen clearly by someone much more experienced than I was. Like the phone call with Eric Bogosian, it was a moment of reckoning.

Olympia was right. Not about the show. The show was wonderful. She was right about me. My real priorities, which I couldn't admit then, were raising my son, being a wife, and mother, hence the move to the suburbs and the slow unwinding of my acting dream. She was right that I would have had to stay in the city for any real shot at a career. And even then, there would have been no guarantees. I wasn't willing to sacrifice my more compelling private roles. Her assessment, of a piece with Eric's, formed a running theme. He told me not to hide in basements, not to waste my time; she told me not to hide in non-professional groups. In both cases, I didn't think that I was hiding. I thought I was making the best of my situation.

Career

A profession for which one trains, and which is undertaken as a permanent calling

16.

I had left the city, but I hadn't left my dream of making it there. Although the dictionary definition of "career" doesn't mention money, I fervently believed that my relentless calling, ambition, and drive would inevitably yield *my* definition: *a profession that pays*. More than ten years after I had arrived in New York, I was still stuck Off-Off Broadway, and it wasn't enough. I needed to make the leap to Off Broadway. Norma Millay hadn't let me attempt it with *A Phrase in Air*, but *Mad Moms* was all mine. I could do what I wanted with it and go as far as my persistence could carry me. I believed a run at that level would put me on the map, get me a theatrical agent, certify my professionalism. It would be an undeniable achievement, one I could point to and say to myself, *I'm worthy*.

To make this happen, my husband and I enlisted the help of his colleague, Victoria, who had ambitions of her own; she wanted to be a theatrical producer. My show would be a calling card for her, as much as for me. Victoria did a very good job of publicizing my Theatre Row run at the West Bank Café (where Ray and I had had our last lunch years earlier.) Although she didn't produce this gig, she actively sought investors for a future longer run.

I had auditioned for the West Bank's directors, one of whom was the comedian Lewis Black. I sat on the floor of their rehearsal space and "did" Rosie Ann, the little girl whose imagination created the Mad Moms, and two other characters. I didn't feel good about the audition. No one laughed. No one cracked a smile. But they did offer to "co-produce,"—give me the theater for free, and we would split the box office. Determined to move forward with any opportunity, I took it. "Say yes"—the cardinal rule of improvisation applied to life as well.

Olympia put me in touch with a director, Elly Huber, who could help me take the show to the next level. The early performances of *Mad Moms* had been directed by my dear friend Kate Levan. She saw me through my bookings at Punchline, at the Celebrate Brooklyn festival, and a filming at Perry Street Theater, which I used for promotion. Kate "birthed" the play with me, a real gift. Now I needed someone to push me to do my very best work. Elly took my performance apart moment by moment and rebuilt it—an excruciating but ultimately rewarding process, which made my acting both more believable and funnier.

Victoria got Comedy Central and Jeffrey Ashe, the Off-Broadway producer of *Other People's Money*—a big hit starring Mercedes Ruehl—to see the show. That was also the night my parents came. I was terrified that my mother would be offended.

For the first and last time in two decades of acting, I had flop sweat. From the moment the lights went up, my face and body were bathed in perspiration, dripping off me in sheets. I was mortified, though only Jerry seemed to notice. And, to my huge relief, Mother loved it. "That's me," she said beaming, in reference to Shopaholic and Laundry Mom. She either didn't get or refused to acknowledge the satiric takedown. All she seemed to care about was the attention that I and the audience had paid "her." She took it as an homage.

Comedy Central said they'd get back to me and didn't. Mr. Ashe told Victoria that I was very talented, and he hoped that *"someone* would help her." But not him.

Undeterred, Jerry, Victoria, and I decided to do a longer follow-up run at a new theater across the street from the West Bank, Café Arielle, for four months, every Thursday night. We were intent on drumming up momentum for the project.

This time, Victoria fully embraced the mantle of producer and got a *Variety* reviewer to attend. Jerry and I still did much of the legwork, but I'll always be grateful to Victoria for providing my brush with public recognition on a wider scale. The review was a rave—*"a comic and dramatic marathon...well-written and expertly performed."* The issue ran all over the country. My show biz relatives, Aunt Doris and Uncle Charlie, read about me in Los Angeles and were impressed. Thank goodness. Next to my parents and my husband, no one's opinions mattered more.

Aunt Doris' acting career had spanned the entire last half of the twentieth century; in her prime, under her stage name, Doris Singleton, she played a recurring role on *I Love Lucy* as the myopic Carolyn Appleby, memorably chased around a sofa by Harpo Marx. Whenever Doris and I spoke on the telephone, her ageless, musical voice sparkled. No one would ever guess her age—she was ever beautiful, elegant, and suffused with positive spirit.

Her husband, Charlie Isaacs, one of my mother's older brothers, was an extremely successful comedy writer. He wrote for and with all the greats in the days of early live radio and early television, including Jimmy Durante, Groucho Marx, Johnny Carson. Before his retirement, he was the head writer on *Alice*, the sitcom based on *Alice Doesn't Live Here Anymore*. Years after *Mad Moms*, Sid Cesar, Carl Reiner, and Larry Gelbart would speak at his memorial.

Victoria, Jerry, and I had hoped that the review would propel the production to the next step, attract investor money, really launch me. But it didn't. Ultimately, my work wasn't alternative enough to be part of the downtown Performance Art scene or conventional enough for the commercial one uptown. I was caught betwixt and between. Or perhaps it was just bad luck.

The *Variety* review hangs framed on my wall, alongside Greer Garson and her eponymous award, posters for the Edinburgh Festival, and photographs of me as Edna St. Vincent Millay, Intensity Jane, and the Queen of England. Another marker, another almost.

17.

In 1990 when the Whole Theater closed, I and many other local theater artists received the news like a body blow. During the following two years, actors, playwrights, and directors met at the Montclair Public Library to discuss the future. Some wanted to preserve the theater space that the Whole Theater had occupied. Some wanted to take it over under a different, less professional banner. I had nothing against community theaters—I had started in one—but once I had trained, gotten an MFA, and my Actors' Equity card, I didn't want to go back to semi-professional status. In my inconsistent way, I was trying to hold out for professional work, as Eric and Olympia had counseled. I had to move forward.

It was at one of these meetings that I met Jane Mandel, a director and teacher, with a professional acting background and an MFA from NYU. She and I stood outside the library after a particularly frustrating session to talk about what we could do next. "Let's start a theater group," she said.

She proposed that we form an ensemble by doing acting exercises together and exploring subjects with which we could create original material. Jane was smart and serious. She spoke in a soft, even voice, which belied her strong, clear vision. Listening to her, I felt that I had found a kindred spirit, one I could trust. Her proposal sounded enticing. This could become the artistic home that I craved.

We met in a room at the Unitarian Church in downtown Montclair. I brought Shari along and Jane enlisted a couple of other women as well. For the next several weeks we worked together as actors, with Jane leading the way as director and teacher. She and I had had similar training in our respective graduate acting programs. We had both done Jerzy Grotowski's "poor theatre" exercises, based on the primacy of the actor and audience, and eliminating all other elements—set, costume, playwright—as extraneous. Many of the exercises involved vigorous repeated actions to unlock the actor's body and emotions.

We also did more traditional theater games, like Viola Spolin's, the mother of modern-day improvisation. The most memorable was Circle Mirror Transformation, which later became the title and premise of an acclaimed play by Annie Baker. We did it almost every time we met. We began in a circle. One person would initiate a sound-movement without words. The others would repeat the sound-movement, transform it into a new one, for the next person to transform. In that way we would continue around the circle again and again. The idea was to make the sound-movement one unified intention, to respond intuitively with the body, not the intellect. We would also pair off and see where that more intimate exchange would go. At its best, the exercise forced the actor into the here and now. I remember feeling alive in the moment and free.

Through these sessions, we got to know each other's strengths and weaknesses. We spent a lot of time talking about the nature of feminism and the women's movement; their impact on us became a natural focus. Gradually, a theater performance emerged entitled, *In the Name of the Woman*. The show explored women's rituals and myths from ancient to modern times.

When we were ready to debut the piece, we realized that we also needed a name for the company. I asked Jerry, who, given his advertising expertise, was good at branding. He suggested "Luna." Jane liked it—everyone did—and Luna Stage was born.

To be taken seriously in the regional theater world, and to raise money, we also needed to incorporate the theater as a non-profit. I contacted a non-profit attorney, who guided me through the paperwork. I wrote the theater's mission statement and articles of incorporation.

It was during this period that my mother was diagnosed with inoperable thyroid cancer, shortly after my fortieth birthday. In the wake of this shocking diagnosis, she revealed that two years earlier she had bled from her mouth. Unexplained bleeding was one of the seven signs of cancer. She chose to ignore it. Had she not, she might have lived; most thyroid cancer is treatable. As it was, she hung on for eighteen more months, longer than the doctors expected.

The stress of her condition and the travel back and forth between Montclair and Georgetown University Hospital in D.C. did a number on my own health. I went from a regular check-up with my New York City gynecologist to the airport, trying to absorb his off-hand remark that my thyroid was enlarged and that I "should get it checked out." I must have turned white. Then I told him about my mom. He said something reassuring, but I vowed not to tell my parents.

As it turned out, I had Grave's disease, a form of hyperthyroidism, which could be cured through medication. (This was the condition I had been assigned to fake for medical students by the prescient doctor seventeen years earlier.) My endocrinologist assured me that the condition wouldn't recur, and he was correct. He didn't tell me, however, that it could have been triggered by "emotional shock," a fact I discovered one evening in my parent's home, when I looked it up in their medical encyclopedia.

With this strained backdrop, my relationship with the theater group got complicated. Shari and I wanted our writing contributions to be acknowledged financially. Though much of the piece had been created by the ensemble through improvisation, Shari and I had written scripted scenes based on current events and pop icons, among them my prose poem on Barbie and her impact on women's self-image. I proposed that we should be paid a small honorarium out of the box office take, say $25 a show. Jane was concerned that money would be too tight to allow a nightly draw.

As the discussion continued, I began bidding against myself. "How about $20?" Jane shook her head. "$15?" Silence. "$10?" No response. When I got to my last absurd number, "$5?" I looked at Shari. She stared at the floor. I sighed.

Finally, Jane spoke, trying to diffuse the tension, handling me gently. She must have sensed that I was on the brink of bolting. "We all need each other," she said quietly, referring to our mutual status as mothers of young children in the burbs, who also had artistic needs. I nodded but felt thoroughly demoralized.

A few days later I withdrew my writing from the show and left the group.

Looking back, I see that my pride, my unrealistic expectations, my disappointment with a stillborn, sidetracked career had nothing to do with Luna or with Jane. I felt terrible about how I left. I didn't realize at the time that I had begun the process of leaving not just one nascent theater company but acting itself. Jane wasn't wrong. The work we were doing was what was available to us, and I should have embraced it. Instead, I ran, because I couldn't reconcile this down-sized version of working in the theater with my out-sized ambitions. I had lived with those ambitions for so long, I didn't know how to give them up for the more modest world right in front of me.

Shari stayed in the group and *In the Name of the Woman* premiered to much fanfare. Olympia loved the production so much that she asked to be on the board. Luna Stage was launched. Jane, to her great credit, turned it into an extremely successful professional theater, known as a daring and nurturing incubator for new works. It is still in operation today.

18.

After Luna, I decided to make one last stab at having a conventional theater career. For a year, I took the bus two blocks from my New Jersey home into the city for another round of auditions. I couldn't put my life-long dream to rest unless I gave it one more try. I decided, rather arbitrarily, that I would do one hundred auditions.

And I went back to class. I needed a place to practice, not as a solo performer of original work, but as an interpreter, the actor's primary job. It was humbling to take acting classes again, fifteen years after getting my M.F.A. and as many teaching classes of my own, but I was long overdue for a reboot. My inner resources had run dry. I needed to recharge and elevate my skills if I was going to give the commercial theater world one more shot. I needed a safe space in which to work out—an acting gymnasium if you will—and to work on myself.

Enter acting coach Sam Schacht, a longtime master

teacher at the Stella Adler Studio, a member of the legendary Actors Studio, and later Dean of the New School's Actors Studio Drama School. Elly, my *Mad Moms* director, had recommended him. Sam ran a private, invitation-only class, also located on Theatre Row, which made juggling my own teaching schedule in Montclair, my theater projects, and family life with my husband and young son possible.

My first session served as the audition. I must have passed, because he said he could see me playing a lawyer for *Law and Order*. Every up-and-coming actor in New York ended up on that series, but despite contacting any agent who was open to new clients, I still didn't have one, so television roles were out of reach.

I found his classes refreshing, because, unlike grad school or college, the students were all ages and from all walks of life. There were working soap opera stars and young people straight out of high school or college, and an older woman—my age now—who had gone back to acting after raising her children. I enjoyed the camaraderie. No matter how different our individual lives were, we all aspired to the same thing—a life as an actor.

And I liked Sam. Unlike many acting teachers of his stature, there was nothing of the self-aggrandizing guru about him. Sam was down to earth, steady, a family man with grown children, and a no-nonsense approach to the business. He had acted in films and on stage. I loved the sensory exercises he led us through at the beginning of each class and his firm but compassionate manner when critiquing our scenes. He had a practical and artistic approach that I knew I could trust.

When I did a scene as the suicidal Jessie Cates in Marsha Norman's *'night, Mother*, which Kathy Bates had originated on Broadway in 1986, with the older actress playing my mother, the studio fell silent. Everyone seemed stunned. I had let the raw despair rip through me, and them. I had tapped pure instinct, and the class recognized it.

"If you are capable of that, you've been selling yourself short," Sam said.

He didn't elaborate, but I understood what he meant. I had long known that I could play serious roles, as well as comedy. My training, my summer stock experience, and the Millay play had revealed as much. But my intellectuality had often gotten in the way of my emotional power because I had been afraid of it. My parents, especially my mother, had labeled my adolescent outbursts "too dramatic," and my "sensitivity" a negative. My intensity and emotionality belonged on stage. *Wasn't this one of the reasons I had been drawn to the theater in the first place?* When Sam validated my untapped resources, I was ready at long last to use and not resist them.

After *'night, Mother*, my view of myself and my capabilities shifted, but the everyday frustrations continued. I still didn't know how to connect with the profession in a real way. Sam understood the struggle. He had witnessed it in his colleagues and students many times. He gave me a variation on the advice I had given my own Montclair State students.

"If there is *anything* else that you can do with your life and be satisfied, do it." The students stared at me, riveted. I rarely held forth with career advice, and they sensed that I spoke the truth. They knew I had worked as an actress in New York City—an Actors' Equity card had been a requirement for the teaching job—and respected my hard-won wisdom. I went on, "Do that other thing, because you probably will have to do it anyway." I was talking about myself, of course. I had "settled" for teaching because I couldn't make a living acting. I stood before them a disappointed actress, giving them acting advice. They sat frozen, rapt. They recognized an authentic warning when they heard one. Then I tossed my young pups a bone. "But if acting is something you *have* to do, you can't live without, then by all means, go for it, and don't look back." I did not take the last part of my own advice. I violated it with every word in this memoir. But I did follow the main charge. I certainly went for it.

After I shared where I lived and what my life was like, Sam said, "It's easier to be a writer living outside the city than to be an actor going back and forth for auditions and jobs. You might want to wait until you are older, 'til your son is grown, to go back to acting." He had a point. I could write anywhere and did. What he couldn't have known was that once I left acting, I wouldn't go back.

In addition to Sam Schacht's class, I enrolled in an audition course for television commercials—additional advice I'd given my students, which I finally took myself.

"Get work in television—commercials, soaps—whatever. That's where the money is. Then, after you have a reputation on the small screen, you can indulge your theater habit." I had been so completely focused on theater that I had neglected the possibility of applying my performance skills to making some real money in the far more lucrative on-camera marketplace. I couldn't walk away unless I gave it a shot.

The instructor was a former casting director for ad agencies—an older woman with a no-nonsense directness. I auditioned for her with a cold reading of ad copy. She seemed more than satisfied. "You should be working all the time."

I told her that I didn't have an agent, nor did I have any on-camera experience, though I'd done a bit of voice-over and radio. She said that after a few weeks with her, all that would be rectified.

Our class was small, five people, with plenty of time for each of us to practice before her cameras. We learned to analyze a script for the key words to punch—a very similar process to the textual diagramming I'd taught at the University of Texas.

"Slate your name," she ordered from behind the tripod. We had been given ten minutes to mark and memorize a thirty-second commercial script. I looked at the lens and began with my usual high energy, though the sensation of "connecting" with a camera rather than another actor felt odd. When I was finished, she turned to the rest of the class and said, "That's how it's done."

After our final session, she gave me the name of a reputable agent who trusted her judgment. "Good luck," she said. "You can do this."

The agent liked my curly-haired smiling headshot and my cold reading, and quickly categorized me as "ethnic," good for "mom" commercials selling laundry detergents and food. "I will be happy to take you on a freelance basis." That meant she wasn't going to sign me for an exclusive contract until she saw how I did at the auditions she sent me out on. She cautioned that it might take one hundred auditions to land my first job—the industry average. Her representation, albeit freelance, was the closest I had gotten to a legitimate business relationship with someone who could help me get work—certainly more legit than the shady management duo ten years earlier.

I sent her my headshot photo-postcards every two weeks to remind her that I was still available—the pre-internet/email way actors stayed in touch with the industry's gatekeepers. She sent me on a total of two auditions, neither of which I booked. She never called me again. I beat myself up, thinking that I wasn't good enough, "commercial" enough for commercials.

A few years later, one of my private students interviewed with the same agent. The young actress had listed me on her résumé—standard practice to show you had professional training. The agent saw my name, and told the student, "Roselee is an excellent actress." By then I was long past trying, but I sent the agent a note anyway. After all, she had remembered me—no small thing, considering the deluge of wannabes she dealt with daily. No response. *What did I conclude from all this?* That it's a numbers game. An agent had dozens of signed clients, whom she had to place first to pay her bills and theirs, and probably dozens, even hundreds, more freelancers—too many to give a fair shot to any one of them. She didn't drop me because I didn't land one of the two jobs I'd auditioned for; she dropped me because I wasn't and couldn't be her priority.

I scanned the spreadsheet I'd created to keep track of my auditions. I got called back a few times, but never got cast. At number 98, 99, or 100—I can't remember which—I looked at the hours-long line for an unpaid Off-Off Broadway play, and thought, *why am I wasting my time?* I walked back to Port Authority, got on the bus to Montclair, and went home to my husband and son.

It was then that I began to consider, consciously and seriously, leaving acting.

I had wanted to be an actress since childhood, but I had to admit that it wasn't working. This private admission—unlike the one I blurted and retracted in front of my parents when I was just starting out—had the weight of experience. Though I had always looked younger than my years, I was squarely in middle-age, and couldn't pretend that my "big break" was just around the corner. I fought the inexorable changes happening inside and out, but they had a kind of inevitability. Once the tectonic plates of my thinking, feeling, and physical selves began to shift, I couldn't move them back to where they began. I had changed. *I no longer wanted to be an actress.* The realization shocked me. *Hadn't I thought of myself as an actress since before I could read? How could I abandon my life-long dream?*

    I could only do so once I understood that it had abandoned me. I had peeled away the layers of ego that had fortified my youthful grandiosity. I had grown up and away from the girl who only wanted to be on stage. So, I did what I knew how to do: I poured my dissatisfaction into writing my first ensemble play, *Rehearsing for Oscar*. Like *Mad Moms*, it consisted of a series of multi-character monologues, linked by one unifying character—in this case, Ruthie, (named after Ruth—"never face facts"—Gordon), a narcoleptic actress, dreaming the frustrating iterations that a career can take, and in her waking moments rehearsing her acceptance speech for her Oscar. Naturally, I played Ruthie. It was cathartic to confess in character, in front of an audience every night:

    "I ask myself, is this what I want? A statuette? An award? A manufactured token?! And I have to admit. Yes, YES, I WANT THE DAMN THING! I—want—it. I want to be showered with every accolade, every tribute, yes, even the Oscar! I know, I know, I'm still scrubbing urinals Off-Off Broadway. It doesn't matter, it's what every actor wants—the star of the high school musical, the community theater walk-on, the perennial understudy—everyone wants to be recognized. We all have the same dream: we want to be GREAT!"

    I find it curious that I didn't call the play, *Rehearsing for Tony*—since it was about theater artists. At the time, no alternative title crossed my mind. Now I think that my encounters with actresses who had reached the pinnacle—film stardom, Oscar recognition—had seeped into my subconscious and set the bar tantalizingly and impossibly high. Meryl, Jean, Greer, Beatrice, and Olympia represented a collective North Star. Hence, "Rehearsing for *Oscar*."

A new Montclair women's theater group wanted to do a weekend of both *Mad Moms* and *Rehearsing for Oscar*. I said yes, if I could cast *Moms* with other actresses, including a child performer for Rosie Ann. I was done with wearing all the hats. The multi-actress version of *Mad Moms* didn't work as well as *Rehearsing for Oscar*, despite the amazing performance of Shari's daughter Ariel as Rosie Ann, but it was an interesting experiment.

Oscar, attracted some terrific talent to play the Crazy Usher, the downtown Performance Waitress, the Suburban Stripper, the last of whom knew an Off-Broadway producer, who loved the show and was happy to lend his name, "for half the proceeds of whatever came out of it." The man must have thought I was totally naïve. He had no intention of investing any money, and therefore wasn't taking the risk a real producer would. *So why would he deserve to reap the rewards?* I said thanks, but no thanks.

Before "producer-gate," I told this actress that the show was my way of writing myself out of the business. She was shocked. "No. It's just the beginning," she said.

Eighteen years after earning my Actor's Equity Card, it was more like the beginning of the end.

The ensemble did two more Off-Off Broadway runs of *Oscar*—one at the Houseman Studio on Theatre Row (at that point my home base) and at the Sanford Meisner

Theatre on 11th Avenue. Jerry produced a beautiful threefold brochure for investors, complete with quotes from The Pasadena Playhouse and Seattle's ACT, respected regional theaters, which read and liked the play, but never produced it. I got a nibble from Smith & Krause, a monologue publisher. Nothing happened.

I wouldn't perform under contract as a professional actress in a play ever again. I had given my theater career everything I had. If I couldn't attract "other people's money," I knew that it was time to move on. The fight had left me bruised, but I had finally grasped what Eric Bogosian and Olympia Dukakis had tried to tell me, that it was better not to work at all, than in half-baked conditions. I couldn't bring myself to want less: an occasional role in a play, a big fish in small pond life in community theater. I had trained for the big leagues and didn't know how to downsize my ambition. Better to retire.

Acting was my first and most passionate artistic love, but first love isn't necessarily mature love. I have often thought that I should have walked away sooner, when I found myself living for the once or twice a year I could be on stage. I was like a free diver—those intrepid souls who deep sea dive without equipment, who hold their breaths for inordinately long periods, risking lung explosion and death, but return to the surface to do it all over again. I gulped each moment of success, held it, because I knew it would have to last me for an unknown, but inevitably extended stretch until I could come back to the surface and inhale the next life-saving breath. My paid bookings didn't amount to a living, but a few dollars along with the thrill of a performance coming alive on stage kept me hooked. It wasn't healthy. I had clung to my childhood dream well into middle age. I was forty-three years old at the time of my last performance as Ruthie. From my secure perch over twenty-five years later, it looks like a classic midlife crisis. But sometimes, a crisis is the only means of resolution. Now I know that my trajectory couldn't have gone otherwise. I had to write myself out to understand and accept why I had to move on. Writing *Rehearsing for Oscar* and mounting its productions freed me. If *Mad Moms* helped me to get over my fear of motherhood, *Rehearsing for Oscar* allowed me to face my disappointment and heartbreak over a career that didn't manifest, and to do it with laughs. It also took many hours of self-help workbooks—*Creating a Life Worth Living*, *The Artists Way*—journaling in a dozen diaries, creating a new vision board—the old one featured a magazine cutout of the words "Broadway Star"—as well as actual therapy, to accept reality and to forgive myself.

By this time, I had been working at Montclair State as an adjunct in the drama department for six years—a period that overlapped with *Mad Moms*, Luna Stage, *Rehearsing for Oscar*, and my mother's death. As I wrestled with myself during my classes with Sam, my stint with the agent, my ongoing efforts to get my original work produced, and the one hundred auditions yielding a few callbacks but no jobs, I started to feel like an impostor in the classroom. *Who was I to teach an art that I no longer practiced?*

After I left acting, I went on "honorable withdrawal" from Actors' Equity Association. The union assured me that I could come back any time, just by paying current dues. I knew, despite my pain at the finality of it, that I would not. And I realized that I was burning out as an instructor; I couldn't be helpful to my students if I taught from a jaded perspective. I was also frustrated by the nature of part-time university work. Full-time posts came and went, but I was never be considered for them; adjunct work was a dead end. Two years later, in 2000, I gave my notice. The department chair wasn't surprised. "We knew we'd eventually lose you."

I had already taken Sam Schacht's advice, and had started a multi-genre writing group in my living room—my version of Olympia's Gathering—which would become a 501 c3 non-profit, Tunnel Vision Writers' Project, Inc. In much the same way I had written myself out of acting with *Rehearsing for Oscar*, I imagined myself in a new role as Tunnel Vision's founding director. The fresh focus helped to ease a lingering grief for my unfulfilled life in the theater.

And for my mother.

19.

Ten or twelve little boys and girls ran around the open room—four-year-old Ollie among them—each dressed in cute play outfits—shorts and tee shirts, ruffled tops for the girls and stripes for the boys. None of the children were older than Ollie; the atmosphere carried a whiff of anarchic chaos. On the periphery stood the mothers, I among them—the stage moms. Unlike our children, oblivious about the import of the day, our nerves worked overtime. In a moment the photographer would enter, choose which children he wanted for this magazine shoot, and then the rest would leave. Only the moms would understand the sting of rejection. The children would interpret it as a play date cut short.

 I hadn't ever planned on being in this position, or for Ollie, my darling boy, to be here either. Every parent thinks their child is special, and Jerry and I were no exceptions. With my husband's career in advertising and mine in theater, we were perhaps better able to approach the world of child modeling than most. I was reluctant, but Jerry, spurred on by an agent on one of his client shoots, thought we should see where it went. "Could be college money," he ventured.

Jerry had headshots made for Ollie by a photographer friend. I had to admit that they were adorable—our son in all his chubby-cheeked, bright-eyed glory—but this whole enterprise was a bit too déjà vu for me. I was in my late thirties then, still pursuing my frayed acting dreams. Every few years, I updated my own headshots, agonizing over whether or not the photographer had gotten just the right angle, whether my make-up was too ordinary, not glam enough, or the reverse, if my shirt collar said "serious actor," if it framed my face correctly, and whether my expression would pull in the viewer—meaning agent, casting director, or more likely assistant—in the nanosecond they would spend looking at it before tossing the picture into the wastebasket. Putting my innocent son through this, even unaware as he was, felt wrong.

We met with the agent anyway. Ollie sat on my lap and played with a stuffed toy, while she laid out the possibilities. "I see a lot of cute children, but your son is beautiful." Jerry and I looked at each other, proud and embarrassed in equal measure, since our genes in random assemblage were responsible, not us. She proceeded to send Ollie to the magazine look-see.

Ollie was chosen, along with a few other children. I don't remember how much they paid him. We never saw a copy of the print ad; it ran in some Midwestern circular. I do remember the looks on the mothers' faces whose children *weren't* chosen— disappointed, pissed, crushed. I would have been relieved. I couldn't see myself carting my little boy to auditions for jobs he couldn't chose and didn't understand. Afterwards, I told Jerry that we would table this until Ollie was old enough to know what he wanted. Unlike me, he hadn't pointed at a television screen and declared his intentions. Until he did, I would retire as "stage mom."

As it turned out, Ollie played leads in school plays. There was a particularly memorable turn as Romeo in the seventh-grade production of *Romeo and Juliet*, but he never made the declaration. Much later, he tried his hand at stand-up comedy, just as I did. My son was way better at it than I was but identified more as a writer than as a performer. He knew who he was far earlier than I had and recognized that he didn't crave a performer's life enough to willingly put up with its indignities.

I sat in my parent's bedroom on the edge of the bed where my mother spent most of her last months. By now I was almost inured to the job of cleaning her tracheotomy tube—almost, but not quite. I swabbed the edges of the raw wound with peroxide and slowly inserted a long Q tip into the white tube to pull out the thick mucus that accumulated non-stop. Since her doctors had informed us on her last day in the hospital that the cancer had spread to her lungs and brain, that it was indeed terminal, all Mother had wanted was to go home.

I walked beside her as an aide pushed her wheelchair through the hallway in Georgetown University

Hospital, where she had lived for months the previous year during arduous rounds of radiation, past the nurses who knew her and knew that we were bringing her home to die. Their faces reflected sadness, compassion, and the weariness of professional caregivers who witness such exits every day. But for my family, this wasn't every day. Mother was the center of our home and our psyches.

My father had reluctantly agreed to allow a hospice nurse into the house. While the nurse took care of Mother, I walked down the hall to what used to be my brother's room. There sat my father, lost and bewildered. He looked up at me through his thick glasses, and asked, "Do you think she can get better?" My erudite father couldn't grasp the fact that his young bride—she was nineteen and he thirty-two when they married—was dying, that she would go before him. His eyes implored me to give him hope, to lie.

"I don't know, Daddy. She's very, very sick. That would be a miracle." He bowed his head.

When I went back to the bedroom, the hospice nurse asked if I could stay. I said that I had to return to New Jersey, just to get some clothes, but that I would come back in three days. Mother raised her head from its perpetual slump and gave me a look, much like my father's. *Please don't go.* Then she scribbled the same on her notepad. I knelt beside her and took her hand. "I'm coming back on Sunday."

On Saturday, while at home in Montclair, I got a call from my brother. Mother had had a heart attack after walking down the hallway with my brother and father holding her up. It was a forced march each day, one she began resisting as soon as she came home. My father begged her to do what the nurses said, to keep up her strength. But she had none. I sank to the floor. I shouldn't have left. I should have been there.

At the time, I wasn't fully aware of how my mother's death had affected my ambitions. As I've said, Leone Isaacs Blooston was not a stage mother with theatrical ambitions of her own. She didn't drag her daughter to auditions, not only because she couldn't drive, but also because she didn't want me to grow up too fast. She wanted me to have a full, unencumbered education. She wanted me to have a childhood. She wanted, above all, for her children to have the stability she had missed, as a daughter of divorce and poverty. I was the one who declared my intention to act by pointing at the television set, long before I knew what the profession entailed. She was responsive, supportive, and encouraging, but didn't cross the line into complete control. Only much later, did I recognize that her joy at my pursuit kept me going a lot longer than I would have continued otherwise. I wasn't an actress *for* her. I was an actress for me. Still, her support steeled me against all that should have forced me to face my failures.

Mother's death had a profound and final impact on my trajectory. I premiered *Rehearsing for Oscar* only two months later. I mourned my dead career and my dead mother deeply and simultaneously. Without her, I had to finally confront the fact that my so-called acting career demanded too much effort for too little return. I missed her and I missed the "me" who called herself an actress. *Without the theater who was I?* For a long while, I didn't quite know, but out of that double grief came a truer, more honest relationship to my creativity. When both my mother and my actress-self died, a new calling—one that had been there all along—flourished.

Success

*A favorable or desired outcome;
the attainment of wealth, favor, or eminence*

20.

In 1998, during an early meeting of the writers' non-profit I had formed, Tunnel Vision Writers' Project, held in my Montclair living room, I told the assembled women—poets, short story writers, memoirists—that I was a playwright. I didn't say "actress-playwright." This marked a big change. As I listened to the writers share their work, I remembered my very first recognition as a writer in junior high school. My English teacher entered five of my haikus in the Junior Scholastic Writing Competition, a national contest, for which I won an Honorable Mention, and one of the reasons I had been so taken with Edna St. Vincent Millay.

Tunnel Vision facilitated my transition out of theater—I still longed for community—but ultimately it became another too-much-effort-too-little-reward proposition. I produced seventeen performance events in seven years, including successful collaborations with visual artists, musicians, and dancers. For each event I did all the publicity, wrote extensive programs, secured grant funding, directed, and curated the programs, and sometimes exercised my performance chops by reading aloud my poetry, stories, or performances pieces. After 9/11, I put together *Future Feminine*, a concert collaboration with musicians, in which I performed my "Worry Rant," and wrote the lyrics for a lullaby entitled, "Baby Girl Born September 11, 2001," sung at memorial services throughout the tri-state area. I subsidized Tunnel Vision with my time and energy. It was a lot, and much like my solo shows, Jerry and I supported the organization financially. Eventually, the enterprise became too costly in every way.

"Think what you could do if you applied all the energy you are giving to other people's writing to your own," my husband said.

When Tunnel Vision's skeletal board of directors balked at paying me ten thousand dollars a year for my efforts—money they would have had to raise—I knew that the entire enterprise was over. I freed myself to focus wholly on my own work, reinventing myself yet again.

I turned my full attention to writing—the core drive that I had long taken for granted. I had always loved words—reading them, saying them, (my childhood nickname was "Chatty Cathy")—and I loved creating something from nothing. Actors interpret and respond; writers create and initiate. Actors have little control, little agency, except on stage; they wait to be chosen to practice their craft. Writers can write anywhere, anytime. For all the out-of-body highs I had experienced as an actress, I sensed that as a writer, I could be a happier person with a saner life. (Sam Schacht had intimated as much.) By embracing writing, by making it my primary art form, I felt far less vulnerable than I had as an actress. I didn't have to face rejection in person the way I did during auditions. Readers, literary agents, publishers, reviewers could weigh in at a remove. To be sure, a writing life included plenty of rejection and frustration, but my years doggedly pursuing an acting career had steeled me, toughened me up. I could take it. I was relieved to let go of what wasn't working and to embrace a skill I had possessed all along. I had a voice and a point of view, and I resolved to use them.

My shift from the ephemera of theater to the concreteness of the written word also addressed my need for legacy—not in the grand sense of immortality, but to reach more people than those who happened to witness any given performance. I wanted my creations to last more than one night. I was naïve about the publishing world, but even given the collapse of big publishers and the rise of Amazon, a book was still a book, and Kindle or print, it had the potential to travel further and for longer than any play. I applied my hard-won sense of worth and professionalism to the vow that I wouldn't self-publish. I finally understood that to get recognition and respect, I had to first recognize and respect myself.

I realized that, like the writers in my group, I could write short stories. And essays. And a novel. And a memoir. I began to imagine a freelance career as a magazine writer. A few years later, with the help of a friend and editor I met in a novel writing workshop, that new dream came true, as did all the others.

Without flinching, without apology, or embarrassment that I might be unmasked as a fraud, I owned my new identify——not actress/playwright/teacher/arts administrator—but *writer*, period. I redefined the terms of my success—the "favorable or desired outcome" — from roles on stage to publications in print. When that day came, and I held my first book in my hand, I became an author, a turn of events my younger self would never have imagined, and a most gratifying surprise.

21.

The Powerhouse Theater at Vassar celebrated its 28th summer in 2013—my first as a Hudson Valley resident. The program developed new plays, protecting them from the critical eye of New York City critics. Its reputation grew and it is now a mecca for professional playwrights—John Patrick Shanley tested his plays there—as well as for directors, actors, and aspiring students in the internship program. Had the Powerhouse been around when I was a Vassar drama major in the early '70s, I'm certain that I would have jumped at the chance to participate.

Although I had previously lived only ninety minutes away from Poughkeepsie, I never made the trek to see a show at the Powerhouse. This was partly out of inertia, partly out of exhaustion from juggling my roles as wife, mother, teacher, performer, playwright, and mostly out of professional jealousy. I knew that I would measure myself against the Broadway actors who were having their quiet summer theater experience on my old turf. Even in my early thirties, I knew that although I had professional credits, I would find myself lacking against their larger public accomplishments. My inner demons and my shame at failing had kept me away.

When I moved to Red Hook, north of the college and in the same county—long after I had stopped acting—I suddenly wanted nothing more than to see a Powerhouse show. There's something to be said for age.

Just as I arrived at the theater, I bumped into two friends from New Jersey, both playwrights. We chatted and they remarked how relaxed I looked. I was glad to hear the affirmation. The Hudson Valley agreed with me, and it showed.

I entered the space, one I hadn't been in, except for at a class reunion, where I, along with a couple of my drama department classmates had snuck into the newly renovated Avery Hall. We stood on the stage, its original footprint intact, and viscerally relived our college productions—*Camino Real, Lady Precious Stream, The House of Bernarda Alba*. We celebrated the memory of their innocence and aspiration.

The Powerhouse was just that when I was in school, a rumbling behind-the-scenes engine room. The intense young interns taking tickets reminded me of my collegiate self, earnest and full of yearning for their life in the theater to begin. The small theater was packed with avid locals and producers looking for their next investment. I had come to see *The Babylon Line* by Richard Greenberg, featuring Josh Radner and Julie Halston and was eager to see a show about which I had no preconceived ideas.

The play, which told the story of a struggling writer teaching an adult education writing class, his preconceptions, resistance, and ultimate transformation, resonated. The writing and performances were top-notch. I couldn't remember when I had enjoyed a play as much. But I took away more than a rewarding theater-going experience. I felt something specific and personal. As I entered and later left the theater, I passed through the old Avery façade, lovingly preserved, into and out of an entirely new state-of-the-art theater. Though I'd never trod those exact boards, I had been in the vicinity. I felt connected, as though I were this production's departmental grandmother, and everyone on stage and behind it was my theatrical descendant.

I had been fully present as a member of the audience, where I now belonged. I didn't think, *I should be up there acting* or wished I had written the plays—no envy, no competition, only appreciation that the next generation of theater artists could offer such substance, and profound appreciation for my start on these grounds.

Over the years, I have had many dreams about Meryl—some filled with laughter, fun, and affectionate ribbing, and some competitive, in which I felt small, though safe in her presence, and guided by her, like a little sister. In the last dream I can recall, she was a peer, a woman in her fifties with children, like I was. We talked about ordinary things. I was completely comfortable. We acknowledged that we had gone to Vassar together, but unlike then, now we could be friends. I felt no need to compare accomplishments; I felt equal. The dream was lucid—I was aware I was dreaming—and aware that this was the happiest connection I had had with Meryl. I wanted the dream to go on and on.

When I woke up, I knew immediately what it meant: that I was at peace with myself, that I'd come into my own. It was a success dream. I used to ask myself *can I succeed?* Then: *can I let go of the world's definition of success to honor my actual achievements?* I wrote this memoir to answer that gnawing question, and in the process to accept my stubbornness, earnestness, and delusions, and to redefine the terms by which I have lived and worked. Most theater artists never make it; most quit early. I didn't, and paid a price, but learned a great deal. Real success is accepting oneself.

I can look back with compassion for my college girl self. She had big ambitions, but she didn't know herself. When I see Meryl now, on screen or in a red-carpet interview, I think, "She looks well, happy, and sane." She did something most of us weren't meant to do, and she did it with strength, grace, and composure. It's taken me a long time to forgive my failures and to embrace my successes. I understand that the scale of achievement matters less than the integrity of the effort, and I like to think that Meryl and I have that, at least, in common—not what Clint meant when he linked us in his fateful pronouncement—but I'll take it.

Artist

One who professes and practices an art in which conception and execution are governed by imagination and taste; an adept or skilled public performer or entertainer: artiste

22.

As in the definition of "career," there is nothing about money-making in the dictionary definition of "artist," only imagination, taste, and skill. I claim all three. Gypsy Rose Lee, represented the epitome of an "artiste." But most often, when I think of what it means to be an artist, I think of my mother.

"You were blooming. I tried all night to turn you back into a human being, but you kept growing and climbing as a luscious rose!" My mother had called to tell me her dream. This was years before she lost her voice to cancer. She sounded so excited, as if the image insured my success, as if a dream could somehow prove it. Her enthusiasm moved me; it moves me still. I have kept that blooming rose in my mind's eye all these years, making it my own dream. Despite our struggles with each other, I never doubted that Mother believed in my talent. She believed in my destiny, which we both assumed to be a life in the theater. At the time, the image bolstered my increasingly frantic efforts to break through, to finally have an acting career. *Now I believe the blooming rose represents my resilience.*

Though I dashed off an incomplete draft of this memoir just before my first memoir, *Dying in Dubai,* found a publisher, I began working on it in earnest a few months after I turned sixty-six. I didn't acknowledge right away what is now obvious: mother was diagnosed with cancer at sixty-five and died the next year. She had been on my mind constantly. It was no accident that I needed to revisit, at that exact time, her influence on my work. I couldn't help wondering if she would be proud of me, of my unexpected career as an author. I felt foolish writing those words. *Of course, she would.*

The deeper question was, *did she have regrets about her own path?* She consciously chose to put her art aside to raise three children and to support her husband's career. She did what many 1950s wives did, what many of today's wives still do, what I, despite my '70s awareness did, with the difference that my conflict played out on a larger, societal scale. We who were raised by mid-twentieth century housewives and mothers told ourselves that, unlike them, we would have it all.

In the arts, this was an especially tall order. It was one thing to go to a regular 9 to 5 job, come home and put dinner on the table, do the laundry, and get the kids to bed on time. At least that job paid a living wage, albeit less than a man's salary doing comparable work. It was much harder to justify the juggle when the "work" didn't support itself or anyone else, when you did it simply because you were driven.

When I remember my mother, the image that appears most often is of her standing at a long table in her studio in what used to be our playroom. Once her nest was empty, in her early fifties, she reclaimed this room and reclaimed her art. The table was placed under a large window, for the light. On it, was a butcher-block board, and on top of the board rested a big blank piece of Italian paper, rough in texture, the better to absorb and reflect her chosen medium, watercolor. Dozens of tubes of paint were laid out next to the paper, grouped by color—blues with blues, reds with reds and so on—along with brushes made of mink and sable in various sizes, as well as a bowl of water, and rags to wipe her hands and sometimes to deliberately smudge the pigments in strong slashes. Except for finger-painting with her young children, Mother hadn't painted in twenty years. Instead, she applied her artist self to decorating the family home, to choosing stylish clothes. The artist stayed dormant, until she began again, committing to her vision, to her work. I wonder if she felt as if she had simply picked up where she left off.

She would call me while I was in Austin and say, "I painted this morning." She painted most mornings. She worked fast. Watercolor required speed; it dried almost as soon as it hit the paper. Her mature work was bolder, more assured, and more "opinionated,"—abstract as it was—than her early paintings. By then she had developed a firm point of view. She knew what she had to say.

She knew who she was.

Those late-life works ended up in various private collections and had a few showings—one in New York City—but rather than push for wider recognition, she poured herself into the creation itself without regard for where it might go. This may have been because she knew she didn't have the energy necessary to tackle the art world, to connect with its business requirements. She once told me that her dreams for herself had been fulfilled, although she had wanted more children. "Painting is a personal necessity, not a professional one. I don't care all that much about selling my work."

When she was dying, unable to speak, she wrote notes to me in bold felt pen on small yellow legal pads. A final one: "The last few months, I have felt I completed a life's work. It is the old tradition for an artist to leave a room full of paintings. They are valuable." In the end, a thousand of her paintings sat in huge black portfolios lined up against the studio walls—an amazing output. Those paintings represented her legacy, a testament to her credo: *the work had value for its own sake.*

Immediately after her death, after Jerry, Ollie, and I traveled to Maryland for the funeral, Ollie sat on the floor of Mother's studio and drew, just as he and she had done together, and just as she and I had done decades earlier. He filled the paper with a mosaic landscape of multi-colored shapes, creating a stained-glass effect. In the center of the picture was a small figure in black wearing a beret, back turned from the viewer, walking through this landscape towards a yellow peak at the top of the page, towards the light. When I asked Ollie what he called it, he said, "Granny Goes to Art Heaven." My seven-year-old knew who his grandmother was.

After my career disappointments faded, I let go of everything but the obligation to always do my best work. From that time forward, I would be responsible only for the integrity of my artistic choices, not what the world made of the results. I transferred the sacred stage space to a place inside me from which I could craft my writing. The form of expression had changed, not the drive to create.

Was I Edna St Vincent Millay, the Queen of England, a Texas transplant to the Big Apple, a narcoleptic actress rehearsing her Oscar acceptances, or a crazed mom desperately trying to express herself? I was all of them and more. I certainly wasn't Meryl, Olympia, Greer, Jean, or Beatrice. I learned the hard way—is there any other?—that you can't control where your talent takes you.

I am my mother's daughter. She taught me that creating art in any form was a positive, life-affirming act and a rewarding, transcendent way to live, to understand oneself and the world, and to find meaning, purpose, and beauty. Mother didn't care what the world thought, or if the world thought of her art at all. The money or lack thereof, the public attention or obscurity, was out of her hands. She accepted her limitations and had her priorities straight. Regarding ambition, failure, and the drive to create, my mother and I agreed—only the last really mattered.

"Do you have any recordings of your shows?" Ollie

asked. He barely remembered watching me rehearse *Mad Moms* in our living room when he was four. *Intensity Jane in New York*, *The Queen's in the Kitchen*, and *The Phrase in Air* were all before his time.

I told him that I had a DVD of *Moms*, and some Manhattan Cable footage of my appearances as the Queen and Intensity Jane, as well as a tape from KUT-FM of my interview on Millay in which I recited an excerpt. "There are photos and reviews, but no, most of my work exists only in script form. The performances are gone."

I sighed. I didn't like to let down my son, but no recording could have captured the unique alchemy between a particular audience and what happened on stage any given night. Theater is ephemeral, and that is its poignant strength. Like life itself, film, photographs, and scripts are poor substitutes for the real thing. The impossibility of exactly repeating any one performance, is theater's greatest lesson for life. *Stay present, be fully alive in the here and now. That is all there is and that is everything.*

And so, I have redefined the terms by which I had viewed my life. I've stopped using their meanings against myself. For years, I *knew* that I had fallen short, and I beat myself up over it. *But who hasn't fallen short? No one who has succeeded in any venture has done so without also failing; it's part of the process.* Beckett said as much. I created. I failed. I created again. I have lived with the contradiction: the pain of no/low status in the world, the pride in going my own way.

Time to put aside my shame about money. Money or

lack of it is our society's measure of success. No money, then no success. By the universally understood standard, I was a failed actress. No *follow-your-bliss-be-true-to-yourself* pep talk changed that. Even when I appeared successful—garnering awards and rave reviews, booking respected venues—I knew the truth. Every project, except one, cost more than it brought in, even when professionally produced. No "re-framing" would make my victories other than marginal. The cliché is: *It's not the destination, it's the journey that counts.* I wasn't so sure. Successful people didn't rest on the laurels of their "journeys." They rested on their laurels, period. Still, like all clichés, it had some truth. My journey to "make it" in the theater was, from the outset, my own. My accomplishments were real.

I was a professional in attitude and skill, as I had been told many times, if not in earnings. I was wrong about "failure," "career," and "professional." I had a multi-faceted career—acting, teaching, administrating, writing. I had a calling, had followed my inner compass, had created whatever I wanted, and sent those creations into the world. I didn't succeed in making a living as an actress, but I did succeed in making a creative life. And my life in the theater brought me love, meaning, and inspiration—often from stellar sources. The people I crossed paths with, famous and not, taught me, changed me, and were part of a full and interesting life. Once I gave up on fame and fortune, I could be at peace with simply doing my work. I could move from project to project faster, since I no longer expected that it had to lead somewhere. The work existed. That was something.

Which brings me to "almost." What did it mean? *Only a little less than; nearly.*

I had invested my "almost" with a chasm of space and was heartened to find "only" and "little" in the dictionary definition. Distant as the fulfillment of my ambitions often seemed, I must have come close, at least according to Webster's. And that was enough.

When I was a little girl, my favorite book was *I Decided*. Today it would be framed as an empowerment tale. In the 1950s, it was merely a simple child's story of a girl making mundane decisions all day long. Mother said that after reading that book, I would preface every statement with "I decided" and then act on the decision. I've *decided* to embrace and transform my "almost." My story isn't partial; it is complete, whole. I had a life in the theater, and I'm proud of it.

Epilogue

January 2018. I had been chatting at the Rhinebeck Rotary's weekly luncheon with one of my fellow Rotarians, Lou Trapani, the indominable director of the Center for the Performing Arts in Rhinebeck, when he mentioned that he was always looking for good parts for women. I admit that when I first joined the Rotary in 2014 and met Lou, I was leery of getting involved in local theater. By that time, it had been eighteen years since I'd acted and more than a decade since I'd written a play. It was my past and I couldn't imagine going back. And, as I've revealed, I was a snob about community theater.

But Lou knew my history, that I had been a playwright, and asked if I had anything. I said sure, and a few weeks later he emailed me that *Rehearsing for Oscar* was "one of the funniest and most creative things I have read in a long time, and I have an entire company of female actors who would love to do it."

I was floored. This was the last thing I had expected when I gave him the scripts. I figured he'd think the humor was dated, that it wouldn't resonate, but he didn't want to change anything. "It speaks to a certain time but is universal." I'd never been so happy to be wrong. There I was, in the middle of revisiting my theater life by writing a memoir about it, and the play with which I had exited acting was going to be revived—what a delightful synchronicity.

We agreed to meet to discuss terms. Lou offered me a generous honorarium for the rights, and we signed a letter of agreement for production in January 2019, with the possibility of using the dress rehearsal for a Rotary fundraiser. Many of my fellow Rotarians had read *Dying in Dubai*—they knew and respected me as an author—now they would see my roots.

Sitting in the back row of the theater for the opening of this play written more than twenty years earlier, I felt deep satisfaction as I heard the audience's laughter and watched the gifted actresses of this near-ideal cast portray my characters. And they did it for love of the art, not for money. I was happy to have been wrong about community theater. The scenes triggered strong memories: the senile actress playing Juliet in the nursing room, inspired by my aging out of parts that had been on my acting bucket list, and of course, Ruthie, played now by a curly-haired Vassar grad who resembled me. The performances and the response to them validated the playwright I had become, and the actress I had been—a no-longer-young woman, who had struggled, paid her dues, and turned her yearning and frustration into drama and comedy. An unexpectedly joy. I didn't have to perform this time; that freedom allowed me to feel what was underneath the script's outrage and satire—my abiding love for the theater.

> *Twenty years from now, if it's no more than this—me on stage for you—then that will be enough...because it will still be my work, my soul...and my award.*
> — Ruthie from *Rehearsing for Oscar*

Ever since I saw Spalding Gray in *Swimming to Cambodia* at Lincoln Center's Newhouse Theater in summer of 1986, when I was very pregnant, I had envied the fact that he could get on stage and tell his personal stories, lay himself bare, and not have to hide behind a character (For young people, who may not know Gray, his monologues paved the way for storytellers at *The Moth*.) My envy and desire were sprinkled throughout my diaries, especially in the entries I wrote after leaving acting:

> *October 1999—I still get longings to express myself on stage, but not as an actress playing a character—more as a Spalding Gray.*

> *April 2001—I have moments when I think I'll be a female Spalding Gray at 60—telling stories about my life with a table, a glass of water, and a bare stage...being open in a way I could never have done in my youth.*

Despite my many years as a solo artist, I couldn't back then have brought myself do what he did. It didn't feel safe or even possible to be that naked. While writing this memoir though, I suddenly felt the urge to take the stage again, this time to introduce the book to readers. The urge was surprising and unavoidable. I knew immediately that I had to follow it because the desire had a certain logic. A Gray-inspired monologue seemed like a better, more appropriate introduction to my coming-of-age-in-the-theater story than a bookstore reading. I told my friends about the idea and everyone, my son included, loved it. I became alternately excited and terrified. But that combination of emotions always meant I had to follow through, take the challenge. I thought, *what did I have to lose?*

When I broached the idea to Lou, he didn't miss a beat, "When can you have it ready?"

"By next fall. I'm aiming for my 70th birthday."

Ever the producer, he noted the promotional trifecta of the memoir, the show, and my milestone birthday return to the stage, and said, "Yes. Let's do it!"

Memoirs are about the past, but this one ends with a projection into the future:

Fall 2022. So, there I was, moments before taking the stage of the Center for Performing Arts at Rhinebeck—off by a decade, but still inspired by Spalding—no character, only me, ready to let a house full of strangers in on my wild ambitions, my pedestrian failures, my encounters with multiple Oscar winners, my real achievements, and my relentless and essential drive to create. Finally, I could strip myself bare—not physically like my namesake—but psychologically, the greater risk. I was about to tell my story in all its bumpy glory to a live audience.

It was time.

The lights came up.

I entered stage right.

I had come full circle.

I didn't live there anymore.
I had gone beyond.

Still, it felt like home.

Acknowledgments

There are many people to thank for helping me with this book—first and foremost, the staff of Apprentice House Press: Director Kevin Atticks, who has been a champion of my work, and who accommodated the rushed production schedule necessary to meet the book launch/performance deadline described in the Epilogue, Managing Editor Elle White, Developmental Editor Natalie Misyak, Designers Sienna Whalen and Tyler Zorn, Promotions Editor Hannah Aebli, and Program Manager Chris Kimani.

Though they are now gone, I must acknowledge the following family members and mentors—there would have been no me without them: my dear mother and father, Leone Isaacs Blooston and Arthur Blooston, and my husband, Jerry Mosier, stood by me in my theater quest long after it was reasonable to do so, and the directors and teachers whose influence and encouragement were formative—Clint Atkinson, Paul Baker, Sam Schacht, and Hazel Wentworth. I treasure each of them.

Many friends, who knew me when—both theater

practitioners and non—have cheered, comforted, and commiserated: Lois Atkinson, Nancy Barber, Joan Bogden, Susan Borofsky, Diane Ciesla, Shari Coronis, Pati Leigh-Wood, Kate Levan, Jane Mandel, Nina Manegold, Judy Rhodes, Lily Rusek, Bara Swain, Suzanne Trauth, Robyn Travers, and Celeste Varricchio. Thank you all!

Special thanks to the director of the monologue, Emily De Pew, and to producer Lou Trapani, whose enthusiasm for a book launch/return to the stage (putting it on his theater's calendar without having ever seen me perform), pushed me to finish this memoir, and to step back onto the boards after a twenty-six-year hiatus.

And finally, I want to thank my son, Oliver Mosier, who first recognized the importance of telling this story, dubbed it "Almost," offered invaluable perspective on the final draft, and throughout encouraged me to move forward. He has my deepest gratitude and love.

About the Author

Roselee Blooston is the author of the novel, *Trial by Family*, a Gold Medal Winner in the 2020 Independent Publisher Book Awards, the memoir, *Dying in Dubai*, a 2016 Foreword INDIES Book of the Year, and the collection, *The Chocolate Jar and Other Stories* (2022), all published by Apprentice House Press. Her plays have been produced nationally and internationally. Other publications include *AARP The Magazine*, literary journals, and anthologies—among them, *The Widows' Handbook*. She founded the non-profit Tunnel Vision Writers Project, taught in university and conservatory programs, and lives and teaches in New York's Hudson Valley. For more information go to *www.roseleeblooston.com*.

Apprentice House is the country's only campus-based, student-staffed book publishing company. Directed by professors and industry professionals, it is a nonprofit activity of the Communication Department at Loyola University Maryland.

Using state-of-the-art technology and an experiential learning model of education, Apprentice House publishes books in untraditional ways. This dual responsibility as publishers and educators creates an unprecedented collaborative environment among faculty and students, while teaching tomorrow's editors, designers, and marketers.

Outside of class, progress on book projects is carried forth by the AH Book Publishing Club, a co-curricular campus organization supported by Loyola University Maryland's Office of Student Activities.

Eclectic and provocative, Apprentice House titles intend to entertain as well as spark dialogue on a variety of topics. Financial contributions to sustain the press's work are welcomed. Contributions are tax deductible to the fullest extent allowed by the IRS.

To learn more about Apprentice House books or to obtain submission guidelines, please visit www.apprenticehouse.com.

Apprentice House
Communication Department
Loyola University Maryland
4501 N. Charles Street
Baltimore, MD 21210
410-617-5265
info@apprenticehouse.com
www.apprenticehouse.com

www.ingramcontent.com/pod-product-compliance
Lightning Source LLC
Chambersburg PA
CBHW031259110426
42743CB00041B/739